ACCOMPANIMENT WITH IM/MIGRANT COMMUNITIES

ACCOMPANIMENT WITH IM/MIGRANT COMMUNITIES

ENGAGED ETHNOGRAPHY

EDITED BY
KRISTIN E. YARRIS AND WHITNEY L. DUNCAN

THE UNIVERSITY OF ARIZONA PRESS
TUCSON

The University of Arizona Press
www.uapress.arizona.edu

We respectfully acknowledge the University of Arizona is on the land and territories of Indigenous peoples. Today, Arizona is home to twenty-two federally recognized tribes, with Tucson being home to the O'odham and the Yaqui. Committed to diversity and inclusion, the University strives to build sustainable relationships with sovereign Native Nations and Indigenous communities through education offerings, partnerships, and community service.

ISBN-13: 978-0-8165-5344-0 (hardcover)
ISBN-13: 978-0-8165-5343-3 (paperback)
ISBN-13: 978-0-8165-5345-7 (ebook)

Cover design by Leigh McDonald
Cover art by Martha Samaniego Calderón
Typeset by Sara Thaxton in 10.5/14 Warnock Pro with LL Charlotte, Good Headline Pro, and Helvetica Neue LT Std

Publication of this book was made possible in part by funding from the Oregon Humanities Center at the University of Oregon and the University of Northern Colorado's Fund for Faculty Publications, and by the proceeds of a permanent endowment created with the assistance of a Challenge Grant from the National Endowment for the Humanities, a federal agency.

Library of Congress Cataloging-in-Publication Data
Names: Yarris, Kristin Elizabeth, 1973– editor. | Duncan, Whitney L., 1980– editor.
Title: Accompaniment with im/migrant communities : engaged ethnography / edited by Kristin E. Yarris and Whitney L. Duncan.
Other titles: Accompaniment with immigrant communities
Description: Tucson : University of Arizona Press, 2024. | Includes bibliographical references and index.
Identifiers: LCCN 2023037883 (print) | LCCN 2023037884 (ebook) | ISBN 9780816553440 (hardcover) | ISBN 9780816553433 (paperback) | ISBN 9780816553457 (ebook)
Subjects: LCSH: Anthropology—Research. | Community-based research. | Immigrants. | Social justice. | BISAC: SOCIAL SCIENCE / Activism & Social Justice | BIOGRAPHY & AUTOBIOGRAPHY / Social Scientists & Psychologists
Classification: LCC GN42 .A34 2024 (print) | LCC GN42 (ebook) | DDC 305.9/06912—dc23/eng/20231229
LC record available at https://lccn.loc.gov/2023037883
LC ebook record available at https://lccn.loc.gov/2023037884

Printed in the United States of America
♾ This paper meets the requirements of ANSI/NISO Z39.48-1992 (Permanence of Paper).

CONTENTS

ACCOMPANIMENT WITH IM/MIGRANT COMMUNITIES

Introduction

Accompaniment as Ethnographic Engagement

KRISTIN E. YARRIS AND WHITNEY L. DUNCAN

Situating Accompaniment

This edited volume brings together anthropologists whose engaged work with im/migrant communities pushes the boundaries of ethnography toward a mode of engagement inspired by feminist care ethics, decolonial methodologies, and Latin American activist traditions of *acompañamiento,* or accompaniment. Collectively, this volume contributes to applied anthropological scholarship by challenging prescribed boundaries and dichotomies, such as researcher-participant, scholar-activist, and academic-community member. In so doing, the chapters collected here unsettle received ways of doing anthropology and explicitly address issues of power, positionality, inequity, and the broader social purpose of our work. We also situate this work within a longer trajectory of applied, engaged, and activist anthropological research and within contemporary decolonial and feminist critiques of anthropology, which seek to redress historical inequities within the discipline and beyond. Drawing together an array of anthropologists working with im/migrant communities in various research settings and experimenting with different modes of doing and writing ethnography, the volume represents a collective conversation about possibilities—both epistemic and empirical—for caring, decolonial forms of ethnographic engagement.

Many of the authors featured in these pages originally came together in the fall of 2016, at the American Anthropological Association (AAA) meetings in Minneapolis. There, we attempted to gather our collective responses to the rise of a xenophobic, racist, and white supremacist political moment in the United States, which culminated in the election of the forty-fifth president. Reeling in the wake of the presidential election, we organized a late-breaking AAA session to talk and strategize about how best to support our im/migrant research participants, students, friends, family members, and communities experiencing overt and rhetorical attacks on their safety, health, wellbeing, and very existence. From this initial encounter, we established the Anthropological Action Network for Immigrants and Refugees (AANIR), an informal collective of engaged anthropologists working with immigrant communities. AANIR has continued to meet regularly since our 2016 founding, acting as a space of solidarity, information-sharing, inspiration, and organization. We have shared strategies for creating sanctuary campuses and advocating for policy change; we have offered webinar series; we have organized conference sessions; we have collectively drafted op-eds, policy papers, and position statements together. In the process, we've offered and received care, community, and encouragement. In these ways, AANIR itself has served as a space of accompaniment that helps inspire this volume.

We are mindful of the historical specificity and the collegial solidarity that has given rise to and sustained the ethnographic engagements detailed here. At the same time, of course, troubling xenophobic, racist, and anti-immigrant tendencies have deep roots in the United States, just as efforts to build a more welcoming and inclusive society and polity also have longstanding roots in social movements for civil rights and immigrant justice in this country and beyond. Though we represent a variety of training backgrounds and perspectives, as U.S.-based anthropologists our work collectively responds to and addresses present sociopolitical conditions: entrenched inequality, heightened xenophobia, unbridled white nationalism, and the challenges associated with the COVID-19 pandemic, with its disparate impacts on marginalized and impoverished communities. We have invited all volume contributors to reflect on how the current political and historical moment has inspired and shaped our scholarship and relationships as engaged anthropologists working with im/migrant communities.

The central questions guiding this volume are: How do we understand and enact accompaniment with im/migrant communities? What does accompaniment offer our engaged anthropological work—as research modality, as practical engagement, and as a collaborative option for thinking and writing together and with our interlocutors? While we situate our approach to accompaniment historically within related theoretical concepts and methodologies, we do not intend to provide a definitive account or to foreclose avenues for thinking about accompaniment. Indeed, one commonality across the work of the authors in this volume is our willingness to engage with the uncertainties and discomfort that our shifting subjectivities as anthropologists accompanying im/migrant communities require. We seek to draw forward these tensions, describing how and why our roles may shift from scholar to social worker, observer to friend, witness to advocate. Across the chapters, then—as contributors describe fighting deportations, engaging in social protest, writing reports and editorials, developing immigrant-friendly programs, advocating for inclusive health and social policies, and fostering systems of support for migrants—accompaniment acts as a grounding force, a being-with and standing alongside, a form of care that shifts us away from received ways of doing ethnography into more unsettled but productive spaces of possibility for solidarity and social justice.

Accompaniment both relies upon and engages with trust, a way of building relationships within the social and cultural fields we work and live within; indeed, social relations of trust and care are central to this way of knowing. Accordingly, accompaniment is not merely a mode of knowledge production but an ethical commitment, calling us as engaged or activist anthropologists to action, to take stances in the world in solidarity with those whose lives we seek to understand, to use our positions of relative privilege as resources for the amelioration of suffering, even if in incremental and incomplete ways. Accompaniment, then, is relational, interpersonal, and processual—as a stance of alignment, it requires humility, openness, pragmatism, and an ongoing ability to be critically self-reflexive. As such, a key ontological feature of accompaniment is its variety and flexibility, and each of the authors in this volume engages with accompaniment through different methodological approaches, writing styles, ethical commitments, positionalities, and understandings of audience.

This volume is intended as an invitation to deeper engagement with accompaniment's multiple and intersecting meanings—as fieldwork, research, activism, practice, and epistemic mode. Drawing on histories of applied/activist anthropology, feminist scholarship and care theory, and decolonial praxis, the remainder of this introduction provides key conceptual guideposts to help frame the chapters that follow. First, we outline accompaniment's epistemic roots in Latin American liberation theology and social movements, which have inspired medical anthropologists and others to engage in politicized, care-based ethnographic practices of solidarity. From there, we situate the volume within a longer lineage of applied and activist anthropology, drawing from these fields of engagement with real-world social problems and from a deep commitment to use the tools of anthropology (especially ethnographic research and cross-cultural understanding) to build bridges with im/migrant communities and work toward social justice and immigrant rights. Next, we position our accompaniment work as anthropologists within a broader framework of feminist theory, feminist social science, and especially feminist care ethics. From these fields we are motivated to highlight our positionalities as gendered, raced, and classed subjects, to use our power and privilege as anthropologists to address social ills and injustice, and to reimagine social and political relations in ways that value care and caregiving as productive labor, moral practice, and political action. Finally, this volume adds to the conversation around decolonizing the academy, social sciences, research methodologies, and anthropology. As such, we argue for the importance of upending traditional notions of authority in our field and pressing for modes of research engagement, knowledge production, and representation that undo colonial legacies, squarely address issues of power and inequity, rehumanize the ethnographic encounter, and demonstrate the important role anthropologists can play in discussions of social policies and advocacy efforts to undo harms and promote social wellbeing.

Traditions of Accompaniment in Latin America

Our engagements with accompaniment in this volume are inspired by the tradition of Latin American liberation theology, which has long offered the "seemingly simple, yet radical understanding that there is power in mutual relationships, and that the intentional presence of another, committed to walking alongside, deeply listening to, and collectively responding with action against systems of oppression can be transformative" (Wilkinson and D'Angelo 2019, 151). Theologians Oscar Romero and Gustavo Gutiérrez first proposed acompañamiento as a biblically inspired approach in the Latin American tradition of what has been described as the Second Vatican's call for service and solidarity with economically poor and politically oppressed communities in El Salvador and Peru, respectively (Phifer Nicholson 2021). Amid the 1972–1992 U.S.-backed armed conflict in El Salvador, Romero began a "ministry of accompaniment" to urge people of faith to live in solidarity with and "put themselves alongside the poor" in their work toward collective liberation (Lynd 2012, 121; Wilkinson and D'Angelo 2019, 153). Gutiérrez and others emphasized the ways in which violence and suffering are patterned and rooted in oppressive structures that must be undone (Farmer 2013a, b). From its inception, then, accompaniment has centered nonpaternalistic forms of solidarity: being-with, feeling with, *and* doing with people situated at the margins of power and privilege (Goizueta 2001, 206, cited in Sepúlveda 2011, 558; Lynd 2012). This Latin American liberatory tradition also includes a clear incitement to those with greater privilege to advocate for systemic change, including the creation of "a different social order" in which all can thrive (Farmer 2013b, 35; Wilkinson and D'Angelo 2019, 154).

Acompañamiento and other forms of solidarity have been central to many Latin American and internationalist social movements working toward liberation from oppressive regimes and to end U.S. militarism and imperialism (Weber 2006). Global human rights and social justice organizations, social medicine practice, sanctuary and environmental movements, solidarity movements with displaced and incarcerated populations, social workers and psychologists, critical pedagogies, community-based organizations, the underground movement for reproductive rights, and global foundations have all utilized accompaniment in their frameworks for social justice and social change (CISPES n.d.; Mahony 2013; Moisa and Bailey 2022; Nuñez-Janes and Ovalle 2016; NISGUA n.d.; Prisacariu et al. 2022; Sacipa et al. 2007; Saxton 2021; Sepúlveda 2011; Taladrid 2022; Villareal Sosa, Diaz, and Hernandez 2019; Watkins 2015; Wilkinson and D'Angelo 2019). And yet, accompaniment has received only limited scholarly attention as a conceptual or methodological framework for a humanist-activist social science praxis.

Accompaniment in Ethnographic Praxis

An exception is the tendency within critical medical anthropology to call out health injustice, analyze health abuses as consequences of structural violence, re-center marginalized communities as agents of social change, and use anthropology to highlight the "pathogenic role of inequity" (Farmer 2006, 20). For instance, Nancy Scheper-Hughes (1995) draws on her ethnographic work on child hunger in Northeast Brazil to challenge anthropologists to abandon disciplinary insistence upon neutrality inherent to many forms of cultural and moral relativism. Asking why anthropologists should be "exempt from the human responsibility to take an ethical (and even political) stand on the working out of historical events as we are privileged to witness them" (1995, 411), Scheper-Hughes has advocated for "an active, politically committed, morally engaged" militant anthropology (1995, 415). In this view, anthropology could and should act as a "field of action, a force field, or a site of struggle." Anthropological writing, Scheper-Hughes asserts, "can be a site of resistance" (1995, 420) through which "we can practice an anthropology-with-one's-feet-on-the-ground, a committed, grounded, even a 'barefoot' anthropology," positioning ourselves "squarely on the side of humanity." Invoking traditions of accompaniment, Scheper-Hughes insists that we can be "anthropologists, comrades, and *companheiras*" alongside those we study (1995, 420). This exhortation inspires several contributions to this volume that take humanist and collaborative forms (e.g., chapter 3 and chapter 8).

While Scheper-Hughes's provocations generated heated epistemological debates among some anthropologists, for others it has always been imperative to act in the face of human suffering, and indeed to shape one's work around such action in support of socially marginalized communities. The late physician-anthropologist Paul Farmer represents perhaps the most well-known and highly publicized example of this strain of public anthropology. Farmer long called on medical anthropologists to resist "immodest claims of causality" (Farmer 1999, 4; Farmer 2013b) rooted in cultural difference and instead to locate health inequities squarely within the structural forces, institutions, and political and economic arrangements that render people vulnerable to risk for disease and death. Farmer's work as an anthropologist and global health practitioner directly drew on Latin American liberation theology to address the upstream challenges associated with structural violence, poverty, and health inequalities by enacting accompaniment and practicing "pragmatic solidarity" (Farmer 2006, 27). In Farmer's formulation, accompaniment and pragmatic solidarity are approaches to medicine and anthropological research as well as epistemological claims to position knowledge production in ways that center lived experiences of historically and structurally harmed communities.

Indeed, the NGO Farmer cofounded, Partners in Health (PIH), uses accompaniment as a mode of global health promotion, specifically by building partnership with *acompagnateurs*, community health workers trained by PIH to engage in work such as infant health and child growth monitoring, infectious disease control, sexual health promotion, and gender-based violence intervention (Farmer et al. 2013). As Farmer wrote, "As long as poverty and inequality persist, as long as people are wounded and imprisoned and despised, we humans will need accompaniment—practical, spiritual, intellectual" (Farmer 2013a, 26). The chapter by Hansen and Robles Robles in this volume in particular demonstrates how ethnographic collaboration, inspired by liberation theology's alignment in solidarity with marginalized groups, can be a powerful form of accompaniment with im/migrants in precarious situations.

From our perspective, accompaniment is a way of doing ethnographic work that seeks to align the anthropological project with the lived experiences of our interlocutors; for us, this means people precariously situated vis-à-vis international immigration policies, surveillance practices, and deportation regimes. In this sense, accompaniment can be understood as a method or mode of doing anthropology, a praxis of showing up and being present with the communities and individuals with whom we work and being guided by what is "at stake" for them in any given moment or crisis (Kleinman 1995). What this at-stakeness looks like varies across the chapters in this volume—at times, it may be ontological security vis-à-vis immigration legal status, at other times, working toward health equity or toward visibilizing the voices and experiences of people marginalized by historical and structural violence. In an accompaniment mode, then, we often decenter previously conceived research problems or questions and let ourselves be guided by the cultural spaces and interpersonal relationships into which accompaniment draws us, even as these may shift based on policy changes, power practices, and positionalities.

In this sense, accompaniment interfaces with ethnography—the hallmark methodology for cultural anthropologists—but also diverges in important ways. As anthropologists, we are trained to engage in ethnographic "fieldwork" (itself a term reflecting an unsettling racist past), a form of long-term engagement involving participant observation, in-depth interviews, and other methodologies meant to help us see the world from the perspective of those whose lives we seek to understand. Anthropologists have long remarked on how this sort of engagement both opens avenues for understanding positioned subjectivity and troubles the waters of objective knowledge production. Indeed, the so-called reflexive turn in anthropology and other social sciences of the 1970s, rooted largely in feminist and decolonial critiques, reshaped ethnographic writing by calling on ethnographers to abandon the pretense of objectivity and to be explicit about their positionalities and the ways in which subjectivities impact research findings. Such insights and approaches are now central to the training of most cultural anthropologists, who ought to be aware of the politics of representation and the power dynamics that ethnographic fieldwork and production reflect and perpetuate.

Accompaniment moves beyond identifying and analyzing the sources of social suffering, and it requires more than an empathetic stance. Accompaniment calls us as anthropologists to act in ways large and small to effect change, to hold space, and to challenge systems of oppression (Carney 2021; Duncan 2018b; Galemba 2023; Saxton 2021; Yarris 2021). This volume's focus on accompaniment in the contemporary anthropology of migration acts as an extended reflection on ethnography itself, on its generativity as a research methodology, its challenges to divisions between researcher and interlocutor, and its demands that we do more than observe those we seek to understand, drawing upon our alignment with lived experiences of marginalization to push for more inclusive spaces, policies, practices—in our academic research and writing and in our pragmatic endeavors in the world.

Accompaniment and Applied-Activist Anthropology

Our engagements as anthropologists based in the United States working with im/migrant, refugee, and asylum-seeking communities align in part with the commitments of applied anthropology, which—like Scheper-

Hughes's and Farmer's work discussed above—uses the methodological and conceptual tools of our discipline to illuminate and address real-world problems. Anthropology can be "applied" in many ways, of course—as a form of so-called participatory action research in which community members identify problems and develop projects alongside researchers to advocate for social change (Fals Borda 2001; Hemment 2007); as public-facing in reach and/or policy-oriented in scope (Heyman 2010); as collaboratively and reciprocally produced alongside participants (Hale and Stephen 2014; Lassiter 2001, 2005); and as activism and commitment to effecting political change alongside research participants and interlocutors (Carney 2021; Galemba 2023; Stuesse 2015; Urla and Helepololei 2014). In any given project or relationship, an engaged or applied anthropologist's role might expand and adapt according to the needs of the moment. As Unterberger, Himmelgreen, and Kedia (2009) observe, "We are challenged to report, document, and publish, to conduct participant-observation and all of us have gone beyond this role to one of cultural broker, advocate, change agent, or policy expert" in the use of community-participatory approaches (2).

Applied anthropologists bring anthropological tools—ethnographic research and cultural interpretation—to bear in helping assuage "problems" in social worlds in settings from health care to law enforcement to education to media and cross-cultural communication (Castañeda 2010; Pérez 2006; Rylko-Bauer, Singer, and Van Willigen 2006). In those contexts, applied anthropologists often assume the role of cultural broker, shifting back and forth in translational modes, and interpreting languages and other cultural practices across differences of power, privilege, and status. This role is familiar to many of us as we are often called to use our privilege, language skills, and cultural knowledge in ways that may support marginalized communities. Yet, more than cultural negotiation, accompaniment acts as a mode of being-with that resembles and is inspired by forms of solidarity and care (Duncan 2018a; 2018b). As such, accompaniment acts as a form of applied anthropology that unsettles the dichotomous "us-them" relations inherent in the cultural broker role as we draw on our skills as participant observers to engage in novel spaces, whether that be in collaboration with school districts (chapter 2 of this volume), binational Indigenous collectives (chapter 3 of this volume), health care policy advocacy (chapter 4 of this volume), or immigrant rights movements (chapter 5 and chapter 8 of this volume).

We are also inspired by activist applied anthropology, which addresses injustice and inequality head-on, and utilizes the privilege and power of the anthropological positionality to struggle toward social justice (Carney 2021; Galemba 2023; Willow and Yotebieng 2020). For instance, Pallares and Gomberg-Muñoz (2016) draw on queer theory and LGBTQ+ activism to explore the ways in which undocumented communities are marginalized through social constructions of "deviance and criminalization," which emphasize social difference to further stigmatize marginalized groups (Pallares and Gomberg-Muñoz 2016, 9). Their edited special issue examines how immigrant rights activists variously contest or reinforce these social constructions of undocumented communities, often by aligning themselves as researchers within these movements in ways that blur the boundaries between researcher and activist. In other work, Gomberg-Muñoz and Nussbaum-Barberena (2011) have applied a critical understanding of immigration enforcement to research with undocumented workers, showing how immigrant labor leaders seek to counter the fear of enforcement regimes to push toward comprehensive immigration policy reforms in the United States. And Saxton, through her engaged work alongside farmworkers in California's Central Valley, describes how activist ethics and accompaniment can advance environmental justice and health reforms (Saxton 2021). As Saxton puts it, "The ecosocial and emotional labors of accompaniment" are a "means of modeling research as care through the human relationships, social support, and structural change that they can potentially engender, even in seemingly hopeless situations. Being there, even when we cannot change systems and circumstances, can have profoundly humanizing effects" (Saxton 2021, 24).

This vein of activist anthropology demonstrates how anthropological engagement with social movements and grassroots groups can produce important insights into the ways in which im/migrant communities contend with and contest the violence and precarity of undocumentation (Carney 2021; Galemba 2023; Yarris 2021; Zavella 2020). The authors in this volume engage with ethnographic alignments, including trust-building with undocumented immigrant community members (Lopez and colleagues, chapter 6; Vargas and colleagues, chapter 8), moving across multiple scales of interpretation to reveal how immigration enforcement is enacted and leaves lasting effects for health and wellbeing in im/migrant communities. Tacking between the ways immigration policies at the federal, state, and local levels marginalize and stigmatize im/migrant groups, and the impacts of these policies on the lived experiences of im/migrants—in their homes, schools, communities, workplaces, and health care settings (Horton, chapter 4)—is a central analytical tool of activist anthropology motivating the authors here.

Some of us have been involved, directly or indirectly, in organized activist work before or after becoming scholars and academics. Indeed, activist and advocacy organizations often provide essential entry points for anthropological research and engagement with im/migrant communities. Further, the analyses and perspectives of these activist groups can usefully inform anthropological understandings of power dynamics that shape oppression, marginalization, and strategies for organizing for im/migrant inclusion and justice. In this way, as Heyman discusses in chapter 9 of this volume, accompaniment can open spaces for considering theorizing from below and decentering academic ways of knowing. Connected within this activist tradition, accompaniment is a form of solidarity, a way to align with the individuals and communities we seek to understand anthropologically that simultaneously demonstrates political solidarity and a commitment to ameliorating social suffering and fostering wellbeing (Yarris 2017). Nonetheless, questions about the relationship between anthropology and activism persist and are among those the authors in this volume address. We explore the differences and overlaps between anthropological accompaniment and overt political activism, and we seek to make explicit the ways in which our positionalities and prior experiences as activists or with activist organizations shape our alignments with im/migrants and understandings of migratory processes. These are provocations the contributors to this volume explore in the chapters that follow, particularly in part II.

One hallmark of an activist anthropology of im/migration is the ability to critically "read" social policy, interpret the symbolic and material impacts of immigration enforcement and the criminalization of migrant bodies, and to use this anthropological analysis to call for social and immigrant justice. For example, Heyman, in his 2010 analysis of Arizona's state law SB 1070—which targeted migrant communities, institutionalized racial profiling, and entrenched the illegalization of migrants—critically examines immigration policy to call for a more humane vision of community and society, "a positive vision of productive, satisfying, dignified, and contributive community life on the part of all persons, citizens, legal immigrants, and unauthorized immigrants" (Heyman 2010, 6). The work of Gomberg-Muñoz, Heyman, Saxton, and many other applied, public, activist, and otherwise engaged anthropologists exemplifies the bold potential of the field to confront power and injustice and to take a stand in support of marginalized, immigrant, and undocumented groups.

Caring Ethnography: Accompaniment as an Ethics of Care

We embrace a vision of doing ethnography that unsettles the problematic foundations of anthropology and of academic labor more generally. We acknowledge that our ability to pose this challenge stems in part from our positions of relative privilege, including, for some of us, privileges associated with U.S. citizenship and privilege of tenure at our U.S.-based academic institutions (even while acknowledging that tenure itself is under threat in some places). Challenging the status quo within anthropology likely implies less risk to us than it might to untenured faculty, contingent faculty, anthropologists practicing outside the academy, international scholars, or others whose professional status is precarious. We agree that decolonizing anthropology—and the academy more generally—requires a radical rethinking not only of how we do ethnography but of what and how we value; of what "counts" as academic labor; and what systems of reward we employ. Just as "caring labor" is devalued in the political economic world, so too is it devalued in the academy in favor of conventional academic modes of production—most notably scholarly articles in high-impact-factor journals or monographs published with academic presses. Several chapters in this volume, especially those in part III, take this challenge on squarely, offering different voices and modes of writing as examples and possibilities. Accompaniment provides an alternate vision as a form of praxis rooted in a feminist ethics of care, one grounded in universal humanity and explicit acknowledgements of power, privilege, and the responsibilities of our subject positions.

In her volume on the *Ethics of Care*, Virginia Held outlines several key principles that are generative for our engagements with accompaniment as method and ontological practice. Held asserts that care is both a set of values and of practices, encompassing both caring for and caring about, and seeking to acknowledge the diversity of ways in which caring practices occur at multiple social levels—from the interpersonal, familial, social, and global (Held 2006, 41). Careful not to romanticize care, Held clearly positions her moral philosophical approach within a longer lineage of feminist scholarship on care-as-labor, reproductive labor, and caregiving, highlighting that this labor often occurs within contexts of patriarchy and other forms of domination (2006, 4). Further, Held carefully outlines how liberal approaches to rights and justice are based on individualist conceptualizations of persons, whereas an ethics of care centers caring *relations* (Held 2006, 13; emphasis added). This approach can thus provocatively intersect with our anthropological engagements with im/migrant communities, where accompaniment centers the relational dimensions of fieldwork. Further, accompaniment exposes the limitations of liberal notions of citizenship premised on hierarchies of deservingness and access to social and political rights rather than moral and ethical claims to social membership that grow out of relations of care and belonging (Thelen 2021).

In our anthropology-of-and-as-accompaniment, we move care ethics squarely into the realm of the politics of im/migration and citizenship. Feminist philosopher Joan Tronto has written widely about the value of care in contemporary democracies, arguing that care offers an opportunity to reorient our political systems "towards the genuine concerns of citizens" (Tronto 1993, ix). In other words, we can consider how the meanings of citizenship (or, as we prefer in this volume, membership and belonging) hinge upon caring for others; or, to put it another way, the value we assign to certain people (citizen or not) determines the extent to which we view them as deserving of care. Relations between care and citizenship are co-constitutive.

Third World, Black, and Chicanx feminisms have long made similar claims, positioning the privilege of academic knowledge production in relation to larger systems of power and marginalization, and calling forward lived experience as a site of theorization, care, and social justice (Anzaldúa 1989; Collins 2009; Combahee River Collective 1977; Gargallo 2010; hooks 2000; Mohanty and Torres 1991; Moraga and Anzaldua 2015; Schutte and Femenías 2010; Latina Feminist Group 2001).

Cherríe Moraga asserts that in the empathetic turning toward pain and injustice, we can encounter and bear witness to suffering in a way that ultimately transforms self and other in human relationship (Moraga 2015). In response to the health injustice exposed by the global COVID-19 pandemic, and to the ongoing epidemic of anti-Black violence, including at the hands of law enforcement in the United States, the words of Audre Lorde have been circulating among many intersectional activist scholars and social movement workers—especially Lorde's claim that for Black and marginalized Americans, care is an act of self-preservation (Lorde [1992] 2017). In a recent provocative edited volume on Black feminism and care, Aisha Finch asserts that caring is essentially about relationality—with ourselves and with others—and that caring thus "derails the needs of state and capital" by amplifying the value and worth of those deemed marginalized or less valuable by racialized, colonialist, and capitalist value systems (Finch 2022, 2).

This volume highlights the connections between accompaniment and care and explores how these approaches to anthropology with and within im/migrant communities inform our notions of belonging in contemporary societies—especially when dominant political and social discourse is infused with anti-migrant and xenophobic sentiment. As is apparent across the work of the contributors to this volume, such violent and exclusionary political contexts raise the stakes for a caring approach to ethnographic work, and ethnographic insights from accompaniment work in turn can open opportunities for building more inclusive and even caring societies.

Accompaniment and the Decolonial Turn

We contend that accompaniment can directly confront historical inequalities and power imbalances between anthropologists and those made "subjects" of our ethnographic research. In this way, this volume builds on a turn made by Carolina Bejarano and colleagues (2019) toward "decolonizing ethnography," particularly in anthropological work with im/migrant and undocumented communities. To decolonize ethnography, we must decenter extractive forms of anthropological knowledge production and focus instead on the lived experiences of those at the margins of systems of racialized or nationalist political power. Similar provocations have been made by Indigenous scholars who argue that knowledge production itself needs to be decolonized, who recognize the power of Indigenous epistemologies, and who insist upon decentering colonialist methodologies and theories (Q'um Q'um Xiiiem, Lee-Morgan, and De Santol 2019; Tuhiwai Smith 2012). In Tuhiwai Smith's formulation, decolonized research is a "site of struggle" against objectification and dehumanization, an attempt among Indigenous peoples "to escape the penetration and surveillance" of the gaze of Western imperialism and Western science "while simultaneously reordering and reconstituting ourselves as indigenous human beings in a state of ongoing crisis" (Tuhiwai Smith 2012, 41).

Accompaniment can thus become an act of learning *with, from,* and *alongside* those with whom we work, not of learning—and theorizing and writing and publishing and teaching—*about* them (Bejarano et al. 2019; cf Jones and Jenkins 2008). These adjustments require both a shifting of our positionality vis-à-vis our interlocutors and an ongoing engagement with the power and privilege that our positionality as academic anthropologists affords us. As Bejarano et al. (2019) state, decolonizing ethnography requires us to "dismantle the subject/object dichotomy on which all modern science is founded," to "understand and prioritize local conceptions of local realities," to address audiences far outside the academy, to be anti-objectivist and anti-objectificationist, and to "acknowledge the privilege and power that come with assuming the Western academic's authoritative stance and to adopt a posture of humility and solidarity in recognizing injustices and taking part in combating them" (Bejarano et al. 2019, 8).

In an earlier moment of reckoning with the colonialist legacies of anthropology, Faye Harrison and colleagues proposed a series of guideposts for "decolonizing anthropology," including decentering Western perspectives, valuing the contributions of "Third World" and "native" anthropologists, and moving an anthropological engagement with "social problems" from the margins to the center of the discipline (Harrison 2010, 6–8). Furthermore, Harrison acknowledged that the institutional structures shaping academic knowledge production reproduced the very inequities that a decolonial approach sought to rectify. In other words, the ways that academic publishing, tenure and promotion, and institutional power operate to privilege certain voices reproduces the value structures within mainstream anthropology that relegate activist and decolonial approaches to the margins.

Accompaniment as an anthropological approach takes on the epistemological challenge of decentering traditional lines of power, privilege, and inequity. Anthropologist of development Arturo Escobar has long called for a transdisciplinary critique of "modernity/coloniality" that draws on the perspectives of the "excluded other" to reimagine ways of thinking and living that draw upon "incorporative solidarity" with subalternized groups (Escobar 2007, 187). In our formulation, accompaniment sits alongside these decolonial critiques, centering caring and horizontal relationships through practical engagements in the worlds we share with our interlocutors. As such, we position accompaniment as a decolonial mode of anthropology that confronts and ameliorates the effects of structural violence and the legacies of colonialism (Todd 2018), engaging pragmatically with ethnography as a mode of redressing historical imbalances in power, privilege, and knowledge.

We are collectively inspired by challenges to redistribute the power associated with anthropological knowledge production, to explore the in-between spaces where our identities as scholars slip into activism, to interrogate where doing anthropology morphs into political advocacy, all the while working toward fostering forms of mutual care and support—both among ourselves and in our relations with our research interlocutors, as well as our students. Decolonizing ethnography requires dismantling "scholarship in which the lives of cultural others constitute the legitimate objects of scholarly inquiry" or a social theory that renders lived experiences the subject matter for "the interpretive machinery of elite European social theory" (Bejarano et al. 2019, 8). Taking these critiques of extractive social science seriously, throughout these pages contributors engage as explicitly as possible with questions of power and inequality as they play out through accompaniment—interrogating nodes of difference and inequality while probing opportunities for solidarity and social justice.

Our discussion of accompaniment is also situated in the historical context of twenty-first-century reconciliation with racist, colonialist pasts that is reverberating through anthropology and other social science disciplines. Within anthropology specifically, this sort of disciplinary reckoning has led to a conversation about the need to "burn anthropology down" (Jobson 2020), questioning the value and the contributions of a discipline long associated with colonial power relations and racialized forms of inequality. We place this volume squarely in the center of such critiques and conversations, contending that accompaniment—with its explicitly horizontal orientation, its insistence upon ethnography-as-care, its decentering of a priori research problems, and its fundamental challenge to injustice, racism, and inequality—offers an anthropological approach that has meaningful and important contributions to efforts toward social inclusion and belonging.

We argue that accompaniment as anthropological practice can help decolonize ethnographic methods and move us toward more horizontal relationships with the im/migrant communities with whom we work. Broadly speaking, we use accompaniment as an organic, flexible concept that contributors to this volume conceive of, experience, and employ in a range of ways. These may resemble activism, social work, advocacy, companionship, coauthorship, shared narration, political alignment, and pragmatic solidarity. At its heart, accompaniment is a "practice of presence" (Wilkinson and D'Angelo 2019, 151), a form of care that has being-with as its centerpiece. Put another way, accompaniment is a *caring ethnography* that prioritizes presence, solidarity, and social relations. Accompaniment centers care, and as such, it also centers feminist ethics and praxis, troubling the seemingly fixed boundaries between the personal and the political, between social theory and social action. Accompaniment blooms out of relatedness and is driven by what is at stake for those with whom we create relationships in fieldwork.

The authors in this volume have been invited not only to explore forms of anthropological research, activism, and practice, but also to consider less conventional forms of anthropological writing. In this vein, we have invited authors herein to use narrative and interpretive modes that they feel best convey the experiences about which they are writing. This invitation has, for some contributors, moved their contributions beyond traditional academic modes and into other narrative styles, including creative genres and collaborative forms; in other cases, contributors have chosen to write using more familiar anthropological voices. We embrace this diversity of voices and approaches as the chapters in this volume collectively speak to the possibilities of what an anthropology of accompaniment may offer and inspire us to think creatively about alternative modes of ethnographic research, praxis, and writing moving forward.

The Chapters and Voices that Follow

Part I. Accompaniment with Students, Youth, and Families

In the volume's first chapter, "'We've Been There Alongside Each Other Right from the Beginning': Accompaniment as Multivalent and Evolving Practice for the DACA-mented DREAM Team," Christina M. Getrich, Alaska Burdette, Ana Ortez-Rivera, and Delmis Umanzor attend to relationships within the "DACA-mented DREAM Team"—a community advisory board (CAB) of Deferred Action for Childhood Arrivals (DACA) recipients in Maryland—as a form of accompaniment. They demonstrate that accompaniment is often a multivalent practice that is necessarily flexible and adaptive as relationships deepen over time and as people's needs evolve. The chapter describes the varied forms accompaniment took in the CAB as it formed as a vehicle for creating space and fostering sociality, solidified into a network of solidarity and mutual support, and transformed into a vehicle for moral support and fostering pandemic sociality. Chronicling these different configurations of accompaniment, the authors argue that the CAB has served as a flexible and adaptive "third place" for building community, cultivating specialized forms of care, and solidifying a shared commitment to immigrant justice.

Chapter 2, "Acompañamiento as a Critical Pedagogy in Action," examines educational ethnographers Mariela Nuñez-Janes's and Dan Heiman's experiences collaborating with their local school district to create a bilingual homework hotline during the COVID-19 pandemic. The hotline provides academic support to bilingual, mostly Latinx, students and has helped to close the academic achievement gap or so-called learning loss due to the pandemic. However, the authors show that, as a form of acompañamiento, the hotline goes beyond helping with homework to provide bilingual students a source of social support and solidarity. Combining personal reflections and drawing on notes from weekly organizing meetings, the authors highlight the practices of being with Latinx youth and families in times of crisis. In this way, the chapter theorizes acompañamiento as a critical pedagogy in action that allows educators and ethnographers of education to incorporate emergent bilinguals' lived experiences as immigrant Latinxs, open opportunities to engage their critical consciousness, and move toward social justice.

Part II. Pragmatic Solidarity: Accompaniment in Binational, Bureaucratic, and Activist Spaces

Chapter 3, "Mercados Dignos: Intergenerational Accompaniment among Indigenous Collectives in Guatemala," is a collective conversation between members of the Guatemalan Indigenous collective Colectivo Vida Digna Carlos Escalante Villagrán, Anna Grewe, Aída López, Juan Pacay Mendoza, Salvador Pacay Mendoza, and U.S.-based anthropologist Lauren Heidbrink. Reflecting on accompaniment as praxis during the COVID-19 pandemic, the authors contextualize emergent forms of solidarity embedded within a long history of state violence against Indigenous peoples. Discussing their mobilization around the Guatemalan government shutdown of Indigenous markets in favor of large grocery stores, which the government depicted as "cleaner" (with all of its racist overtones), the chapter explores the possibilities of intergenerational activism, binational organizing, and an ethic of collective care centering Indigenous knowledge and practice.

In "'Being-With,' 'Doing For,' and 'Doing *With*': An Accompaniment Approach to Applied Research," Sarah B. Horton draws upon her long-term relationships with two Latina immigrants from her study on Latinx immigrants' access to health care to highlight the forms accompaniment can take when integrated into research—whether a means of empathically "being-with," of engaging in advocacy and "doing for," or of engaging in solidary action with our interlocutors as accomplices. Rather than prioritize the researcher's goals of data collection, an accompaniment approach to research centers the relational dimensions of fieldwork, requiring empathic listening and engaging in acts of micro-advocacy. And yet accompaniment-as-navigation raises thorny questions: When does our role as brokers end? Is navigation sustainable over the long-term? And, in the face of the insurmountable structural violence our participants face, how can navigation ever be "good enough"? This chapter engages in critical reflection on the ethical pitfalls of defining accompaniment solely as micro-advocacy, as the urgency of *doing for* often trumps all when our participants face circumstances of oppressive legal violence. It draws upon the author's experiences working with research participants to reform state Emergency Medicaid policy to suggest that an accompaniment approach to research is most empowering when it can transcend the verticality entailed in *doing for* to instead become a radical form of *doing with.*

Chapter 5, "Accompaniment in Activist Spaces: Solidarity at Ethnography's Edges with an Immigrant Bond Fund," examines the multiple subjectivities anthropologists engage with through ethnographic work in solidarity with immigrant activism. Here, Kristin Elizabeth Yarris explores how power and privilege shape anthropological positionalities, probing the potentials and the limits of ethnographic engagement with movements for im/migrant rights. These reflections emerge from ongoing work with immigrant rights organizing in Oregon, including with a network of volunteers working to resettle asylum seekers and to establish a bond fund to release immigrants from detention. Inspired by decolonial approaches and drawing on abolitionist and antiracist approaches, the author engages in critical self-reflection on her personal engagements with the immigration bond fund to expose the possibilities and limitations of ethnography as methodological praxis and as embodied social solidarity. The chapter also considers how employing accompaniment in activist spaces opens possibilities for understanding dynamics of deservingness and care within im/migrant rights movements in a broader context of state violence and exclusion.

Part III. Methodologies of Accompaniment: Affect, Stories, and Solidarity

In chapter 6, "A Public Health of Accompaniment," William Lopez, Nolan Kline, Alana LeBrón, and Nicole Novak draw on their research and advocacy around the health impacts of immigration enforcement to frame these engagements as forms of accompaniment that are distinct from other public health approaches such as community-based or community-engaged research. The authors have engaged deeply with families and communities impacted by surveillance and deportation through various positionalities—as researchers gathering data on IRB-approved studies, as representatives of volunteer organizations, and as members of impacted communities. Drawing from the Zapatista concept of *digna rabia*, or "dignified rage," the chapter emphasizes that a public health of accompaniment prioritizes building and maintaining human relationships in the face of violence and injustice that, rightfully so, makes you deeply angry. Together, the authors' experiences show how a public health of accompaniment includes sharing all aspects of our identities and family lives, grappling with privilege and inequality, confronting the limitations of research training, and emphasizing connectedness over research output.

Chapter 7, "Accompaniment and Testimonio: Migration Narratives in and beyond the U.S.-Mexico Borderlands" asks: What possibilities do scholar-community collaborations hold for producing knowledge that is simultaneously popular and academic? Tobin Hansen and María Engracia Robles Robles respond to this question, drawing from their experiences crafting a co-edited book of first-person narratives of people's experiences of mobilities and immobilities in northern Mexico. Various notions of accompaniment—in relationships with people on the move or stuck in place; in objectives for crafting and sharing educational materials; and in collaboration, coauthorship, co-editorship, and friendship—inform the authors' approach to community solidarity, migrant justice, and raising social awareness. They explore their trajectories and commitments to people's vulnerabilities in the U.S.-Mexico borderlands—Hansen as a scholar-advocate and Robles Robles as a religious humanitarian—and the project's inception, execution, and afterlife in order to gain insights into the potential for narrative collaboration as a form of accompaniment.

In chapter 8, "*Convivencia*: Storytelling as Accompaniment, Activism, and Care," Erika Vargas, Lupe López, and Whitney L. Duncan intersperse storytelling, *testimonio*, and reflection on the process of coming together—through ethnographic research, activism, mutual support, and experiences of motherhood—to work on a multimodal storytelling project. In this project, called *Convivencia*, undocumented Latina women shape, share, and author their stories in their own voices with supportive anthropological accompaniment. The authors have worked together in both research and activism spaces; in the process, the branches of ethnography, friendship, accompaniment, activism, and family have become increasingly intertwined. Co-produced as an act of care, community-building, and advocacy, Convivencia both reflects and deepens these layered relations. The project draws on multiple traditions—including oral *testimonio* and collaborative ethnography—to center immigrant women's voices. Together, this work blends the personal and political to challenge dominant portrayals of undocumented immigrants and create spaces of solidarity and healing.

Part IV. Concluding Reflections: Accompaniment and Caring Anthropology

In chapter 9, Josiah Heyman provides a commentary, "Accompaniment as Moral and Political Practices: Possibilities and Challenges," in which the author offers a conceptual perspective on accompaniment based on longstanding engagement as an applied anthropologist of im/migration. Drawing out themes, patterns, and insights from the preceding contributions, this chapter situates the volume into broader and longer-standing conversations in applied anthropology and the anthropology of migration.

In chapter 10, "Putting Accompaniment into Practice: Considerations for Students and Scholars," Kristin Yarris and Whitney L. Duncan offer key guideposts and considerations for other engaged scholars of im/migration interested in working with accompaniment as a framework and methodological praxis. These considerations include ideas about initiating research collaborations, discerning the commitments we have to communities we work with, and writing for broader public audiences and otherwise disseminating our work using multiple modalities and forms. This final chapter is both a summary and reflection on overarching themes present in the chapters across this volume, as well as a conversation about doing accompaniment in ways that are accessible for students and scholars across disciplines and positionalities.

In an afterword, Mirian A. Mijangos García and Carolina Alonso Bejarano offer a musical reflection on the meanings of accompaniment as activism, connection, and poetic possibility.

References

Anzaldúa, Gloria. 1989. *Borderlands/La Frontera: The New Mestiza*. 2nd ed. San Francisco: Aunt Lute Books.

Bejarano, Carolina Alonso, Lucia López Juárez, Mirian Mijangos García, and Daniel Goldstein. 2019. *Decolonizing Ethnography: Undocumented Immigrants and New Directions in Social Science*. Durham, NC: Duke University Press.

Carney, Megan A. 2021. *Island of Hope: Migration and Solidarity in the Mediterranean*. Oakland: University of California Press.

Castañeda, Heide. 2010. "Im/Migration and Health: Conceptual, Methodological, and Theoretical Propositions for Applied Anthropology." *NAPA Bulletin* 34 (1): 6–27. https://doi.org/10.1111/j.1556-4797.2010.01049.x.

Collins, Patricia Hill. 2009. *Black Feminist Thought: Knowledge, Consciousness, and the Politics of Empowerment*. 2nd ed. New York: Routledge.

Combahee River Collective. 1977. "The Combahee River Collective Statement." Black Past. Accessed June 5, 2023. https://www.blackpast.org/african-american-history/combahee-river-collective-statement-1977/.

Committee in Solidarity with the People of El Salvador (CISPES). n.d. CISPES. Accessed June 5, 2023. https://cispes.org.

Duncan, Whitney L. 2018a. "Acompañamiento/Accompaniment." Society for Cultural Anthropology. January 31, 2018. https://culanth.org/fieldsights/acompañamiento-accompaniment.

Duncan, Whitney L. 2018b. *Transforming Therapy: Mental Health Practice and Cultural Change in Mexico*. Nashville, TN: Vanderbilt University Press.

Escobar, Arturo. 2007. "Worlds and Knowledges Otherwise: The Latin American Modernity/Coloniality Research Program." *Cultural Studies* 21 (2–3): 179–210.

Fals Borda, Orlando. 2001. "Participatory (Action) Research in Social Theory: Origins and Challenges." In *Handbook of Action Research: Participative Inquiry and Practice*, edited by Peter Reason and Hilary Bradbury, 27–37. London: SAGE.

Farmer, Paul. 1999. *Infections and Inequalities: The Modern Plagues*. Berkeley: University of California Press.

Farmer, Paul. 2006. *Pathologies of Power: Health, Human Rights, and the New War on the Poor*. Berkeley: University of California Press.

Farmer, Paul. 2013a. "Reimagining Accompaniment: A Doctor's Tribute to Gustavo Gutiérrez." In *In the Company of the Poor: Conversations with Dr. Paul Farmer and Fr. Gustavo Gutierrez*, edited by Michael Griffin and Jennie Weiss-Block, 15–26. Maryknoll, NY: Orbis Books.

Farmer, Paul. 2013b. "Health, Healing, and Social Justice: Insights from Liberation Theology." In *In the Company of the Poor: Conversations with Dr. Paul Farmer and Fr. Gustavo Gutierrez*, edited by Michael Griffin and Jennie Weiss-Block, 35–70. Maryknoll, NY: Orbis Books.

Farmer, Paul, Arthur Kleinman, Jim Y. Kim, and Matthew Basilico. 2013. *Reimagining Global Health: An Introduction*. Berkeley: University of California Press.

Finch, Aisha K. 2022. "Introduction: Black Feminism and the Practice of Care." *Palimpsest: A Journal on Women, Gender, and the Black International* 11 (1): 1–41.

Galemba, Rebecca Burke. 2023. *Laboring for Justice: The Fight against Wage Theft in an American City*. Stanford, CA: Stanford University Press.

Gargallo, Francesca. 2010. *Antología del pensamiento feminista nuestroamericano*. Venezuela: Biblioteca Ayacucho.

Goizueta, Roberto S. 2001. *Caminemos con Jesus: Toward a Hispanic/Latino Theology of Accompaniment*. 2nd ed. Maryknoll, NY: Orbis Books.

Gomberg-Muñoz, Ruth, and Laura Nussbaum-Barberena. 2011. "Is Immigration Policy Labor Policy? Immigration Enforcement, Undocumented Workers, and the State." *Human Organization* 70 (4): 366–375.

Hale, Charles R., and Lynn Stephen, eds. 2014. *Otros Saberes: Collaborative Research on Indigenous and Afro-Descendant Cultural Politics*, 1st ed. Santa Fe, NM: SAR Press. muse.jhu.edu/book/35836.

Harrison, Faye V. 2010. *Decolonizing Anthropology: Moving Further toward an Anthropology for Liberation*, 3rd ed. Arlington, VA: American Anthropological Association.

Held, Virginia. 2006. *The Ethics of Care: Personal, Political, and Global.* New York: Oxford University Press.

Hemment, Julie. 2007. "Public Anthropology and the Paradoxes of Participation: Participatory Action Research and Critical Ethnography in Provincial Russia." *Human Organization* 66 (3): 301–314.

Heyman, Josiah. 2010. "Human Rights and Social Justice Briefing 1: Arizona's Immigration Law—SB 1070." *Society for Applied Anthropology.* Issue Briefing, Human Rights and Social Justice Committee.

hooks, bell. 2000. *Feminist Theory: From Margin to Center.* London: Pluto Press.

Jobson, Ryan Cecil. 2020. "The Case for Letting Anthropology Burn: Sociocultural Anthropology in 2019." *American Anthropologist* 122 (2): 259–271.

Jones, Alison, and Kuni Jenkins. 2008. "Rethinking Collaboration: Working the Indigene-Colonizer Hyphen." In *Handbook of Critical and Indigenous Methodologies*, edited by Norman K. Denzin, Yvonna S. Lincoln, and Linda Tuhiwai Smith, 471–86. Thousand Oaks, CA: Sage.

Kleinman, Arthur. 1995. *Writing at the Margin: Discourse between Anthropology and Medicine.* Berkeley: University of California Press.

Lassiter, Luke Eric. 2001. "From 'Reading over the Shoulders of Natives' to 'Reading Alongside Natives,' Literally: Toward a Collaborative and Reciprocal Ethnography." *Journal of Anthropological Research* 57 (2): 137–149.

Lassiter, Luke Eric. 2005. *The Chicago Guide to Collaborative Ethnography.* Chicago: University of Chicago Press.

Latina Feminist Group. 2001. *Telling to Live: Latina Feminist Testimonios.* Durham, NC: Duke University Press.

Lorde, Audre. (1992) 2017. *A Burst of Light and Other Essays*, 2nd ed. Mineola, NY: Ixia Press.

Lynd, Staughton. 2012. *Accompanying: Pathways to Social Change.* Oakland, CA: PM Press.

Mahony, Liam. 2013. "The Accompaniment Model in Practice: Leverage in Action." *Fellowship* 77 (7–12): 12–16.

Mohanty, Chandra Talpade, and Lourdes Torres, eds. 1991. *Third World Women and the Politics of Feminism.* Bloomington: Indiana University Press.

Moisa, Daniela, and Gabrielle Bailey. 2022. "Accompaniment: The Practice of Solidarity, Care, Accountability, and Trust." The Global Resilience Fund. July 28, 2022. https://www.theglobalresiliencefund.org/post/accompaniment.

Moraga, Cherríe. 2015. "La Jornada: Preface, 1981." In *This Bridge Called My Back: Writings by Radical Women of Color*, 4th ed., edited by Cherríe Moraga and Gloria Anzaldúa, xxxv. Albany, NY: SUNY Press.

Moraga, Cherríe, and Gloria Anzaldúa, eds. 2015. *This Bridge Called My Back: Writings by Radical Women of Color*, 4th ed., Albany, NY: SUNY Press.

Network in Solidarity with the People of Guatemala (NISGUA). n.d. Guatemala Accompaniment Project. Accessed May 18, 2023. https://nisgua.org/gap/.

Nuñez-Janes, Mariela, and Mario Ovalle. 2016. "Organic Activists: Undocumented Youth Creating Spaces of Acompañamiento." *Diaspora, Indigenous, and Minority Education* 10 (4): 189–200.

Palleres, Amalia, and Gomberg-Muñoz, Ruth. 2016. "Politics of Motion: Ethnography with Undocumented Activists and of Undocumented Activism." *North American Dialogue* 19 (1): 4–12.

Pérez, Ramona L. 2006. "The Misunderstanding of Mexican Community Life in Urban Apartment Space: A Case Study in Applied Anthropology and Community Policing." *City and Society* 18 (2): 232–259.

Phifer Nicholson, C. Jr. 2021. "Made Known in the Breaking of Bread: Accompaniment and the Practice of Medicine." *The Linacre Quarterly* 88 (3): 281–290.

Prisacariu, Dani, Jody Myrum, Laura Vergara, and Ruby Johnson. 2022. "Sprouting Our Collective Wisdom: Towards a Politics of Practice for Activist-Led Accompaniment: Lessons from the Global Resilience Fund." Accessed May 18, 2023. https://www.theglobalresiliencefund.org/_files/ugd/5774b2_1e3e4b7127164ca1814b1cc81207c80b.pdf.

Q'um Q'um Xiiem, Jo-Ann Archibald, Jenny Bol Jun Lee-Morgan, and Jason De Santol, eds. 2019. *Decolonizing Research: Indigenous Storywork as Methodology*. London: Zed Books.

Rylko-Bauer, Barbara, Merrill Singer, and John Van Willigen. 2006. "Reclaiming Applied Anthropology: Its Past, Present, and Future." *American Anthropologist* 108: 178–190.

Sacipa, Stella, Raúl Vidales, Luisa Galindo, and Claudia Tovar. 2007. "Psychosocial Accompaniment to Liberate the Suffering Associated with the Experience of Forced Displacement." *Universitas Psychologica* 6 (3): 589–600.

Saxton, Dvera I. 2021. *The Devil's Fruit: Farmworkers, Health, and Environmental Justice*. New Brunswick, NJ: Rutgers University Press.

Scheper-Hughes, Nancy. 1995. "The Primacy of the Ethical: Propositions for a Militant Anthropology." *Current Anthropology* 36 (3): 409–440.

Schutte, Ofelia, and María Luisa Femenías. 2010. "Feminist Philosophy." In *A Companion to Latin American Philosophy*, edited by Susan Nuccetelli, Ofelia Schutte, and Otávio Bueno, 397–411. Oxford: Wiley-Blackwell.

Sepúlveda, Enrique III. 2011. "Toward a Pedagogy of Acompañamiento: Mexican Migrant Youth Writing from the Underside of Modernity." *Harvard Educational Review* 81 (3): 550–573.

Stuesse, Angela. 2015. "Anthropology for Whom?: Challenges and Prospects of Activist Scholarship." In *Public Anthropology in a Borderless World*, edited by Sam Beck and Carl Maida, 221–246. New York: Berghahn Books.

Taladrid, Stephania. 2022. "The Post-Roe Abortion Underground." *New Yorker*. October 10, 2022. https://www.newyorker.com/magazine/2022/10/17/the-post-roe-abortion-underground.

Thelen, Tatjana. 2021. "Care as Belonging, Difference, Inequality." Oxford Encyclopedias: Anthropology. May 26, 2021. https://doi.org/10.1093/acrefore/9780190854584.013.353.

Todd, Zoe. 2018. "The Decolonial Turn 2.0: The Reckoning." Anthrodendum. June 15, 2018. https://anthrodendum.org/2018/06/15/the-decolonial-turn-2-0-the-reckoning/.

Tronto, Joan. 1993. *Moral Boundaries: A Political Argument for an Ethics of Care*. New York: Routledge.

Tuhiwai Smith, Linda. 2012. *Decolonizing Methodologies: Research and Indigenous Peoples*, 3rd ed. London: Zed Books.

Unterberger, Alayne, David Himmelgreen, and Satish Kedia. 2009. *Invisible Anthropologists: Engaged Anthropology in Immigrant Communities*. Malden, MA: Wiley Periodicals, Inc.

Urla, Jacqueline, and Justin Helepololei. 2014. "The Ethnography of Resistance Then and Now: On Thickness and Activist Engagement in the Twenty-First Century." *History and Anthropology* 25 (4): 431–451.

Villarreal Sosa, Leticia, Silvia Diaz, and Rosalba Hernandez. 2019. "Accompaniment in a Mexican Immigrant Community: Conceptualization and Identification of Biopsychosocial Outcomes." *Journal of Religion and Spirituality in Social Work: Social Thought* 38 (1): 21–42.

Watkins, Mary. 2015. "Psychosocial Accompaniment." *Journal of Social and Political Psychology* 3 (1): 324–341.

Weber, Clare M. 2006. *Visions of Solidarity: US Peace Activists in Nicaragua from War to Women's Activism and Globalization*. Lanham, MD: Lexington Books.

Wilkinson, Meredith T., and Karen A. D'Angelo. 2019. "Community-Based Accompaniment and Social Work—A Complementary Approach to Social Action." *Journal of Community Practice* 27 (2): 151–167.

Willow, Anna J., and Kelly A. Yotebieng. 2020. *Anthropology and Activism: New Contexts, New Conversations*. New York: Routledge.

Yarris, Kristin E. 2017. *Care across Generations: Solidarity and Sacrifice in Transnational Families*. Palo Alto, CA: Stanford University Press.

Yarris, Kristin E. 2021. "ICE Offices and Immigration Courts: Accompaniment in Zones of Illegality." *Human Organization* 80 (3): 214–223.

Zavella, Patricia. 2020. *The Movement for Reproductive Justice: Empowering Women of Color through Social Activism*. New York: New York University Press.

PART I

Accompaniment with Students, Youth, and Families

CHAPTER 1

"We've Been There Alongside Each Other Right from the Beginning"

Accompaniment as Multivalent and Evolving Practice for the DACA-mented DREAM Team

CHRISTINA M. GETRICH, ALASKA BURDETTE, ANA ORTEZ-RIVERA, AND DELMIS UMANZOR

It was a sweltering summer evening in Washington, D.C., when our community advisory board (CAB), focused on the health and well-being of local Deferred Action for Childhood Arrivals (DACA) recipients, first assembled in August 2017. As we grabbed snacks and sat around the table, the possible DACA rescission already loomed large. Some members were well in the know that President Trump was intending to take action to end DACA, though for others, this news came as an unsettling shock that we then took the time to process together. From its first meeting, then, the DACA-mented DREAM Team (as we named our group that August day) was much more than just a research entity; it also served as a vehicle for disseminating information horizontally and a safe space for providing social support during unsettling times.

The research value of CABs has been well documented in the literature on participatory research to address health inequalities and promote health equity (Hacker 2017; Israel et al. 2005; Wallerstein and Duran 2006; Wallerstein et al. 2017). CABs provide an infrastructure for academic-community partnerships that are collaborative, seek to co-construct knowledge production, and aim to combine knowledge and action for social change. CAB members often share a common facet of identity and are selected based on their lived experiences, local knowledge, and specialized skill sets (Newman et al. 2011). In their roles as partners or advisors (depending on how deeply collaborative the project is), they provide valuable insight about the research topic and advise about the suitability of research processes for the community of focus. They may shape the direction of the research at every stage, from inception to conclusion, including designing the study and study instruments, strategizing about and facilitating recruitment, participating in data collection, analyzing data and validating interpretations, and disseminating findings (Hacker 2017).

Scholars have recognized that CABs are particularly productive structures for collaborating with immigrant and refugee communities due to their focus on trust, respect for community norms, and consideration of immigration-related vulnerabilities (Hacker 2017; Miller et al. 2021; Ortega et al. 2018; Rustage et al. 2021). CABs can be particularly advantageous in addressing mental health trauma and distress related to the migration process, settlement-related stressors, and ongoing legal status precarity (Miller et al. 2021, Stacciarini et al. 2015). CABs are also beneficial with undocumented youth specifically in reckoning with their marginalized status, addressing their lack of access to care, and promoting overall mental health and well-being (Raymond-Flesh et al. 2014; Stacciarini et al. 2015; Sudhinaraset et al. 2017a, 2017b).

Though there is considerable scholarly attention on best practices for the formation, operations, and maintenance of CABs (Newman et al. 2011), less attention has been paid to interactional dynamics within CABs and how they can take on a life of their own over time. In this chapter, we describe our ethnographic engagement with our CAB over a five-year period through the lens of accompaniment. In line with other critically engaged anthropologists, we conceive of accompaniment as an ethnographic practice that cultivates forms of relatedness rooted in mutual respect, reciprocity, and support irrespective of one's life circumstances (Duncan 2018; Nuñez-Janes, Ovalle, and Plancarte 2018; Santiago Martinez et al. 2020; Saxton 2021). In the context of our CAB, we demonstrate that accompaniment is often a multivalent practice that is necessarily flexible and adaptive as relationships deepen over time and peoples' needs evolve. We describe these temporal shifts and varied forms accompaniment took in the CAB as it (1) formed as a vehicle for creating space and fostering sociality (in 2017); (2) solidified into a network of solidarity and mutual support (2018–early 2020); and (3) transformed into a vehicle for moral support and "corona sociality" (Long 2020b, 248) (2020 to the present). In chronicling these different configurations of accompaniment, it becomes clear that the CAB has served as a flexible and adaptive "third place" (Butler and Diaz 2016; Hardy 2020) for building community, solidifying a shared commitment to immigrant justice, and cultivating specialized forms of care.

Accompaniment as Creating Space and Fostering Sociality (2017)

As we initially formed our CAB, accompaniment meant creating a space through which participants could forge connections. We began our research on the health and well-being of DACA recipients in 2016. Christina Getrich (a cisgender, white, U.S. citizen, female professor at the University of Maryland) wanted to continue her research with immigrant young adults living in mixed-status families in her current community of residence where she also grew up, away from the Southwest, where most of her previous research was based. She was also motivated to create a project that would enable her students to gain hands-on experience in applied immigration solidarity work and learn about every step of the research process, starting with gaining approval from the institutional review board (IRB).

The initial research team consisted of anthropology undergraduate students Alaska Burdette, Ana Ortez-Rivera, and Delmis Umanzor, who were then joined by graduate students Kaelin Rapport and Umai Habibah. Four of them came from immigrant families, had social networks containing DACA recipients, and possessed local immigrant community knowledge. Their contributions were invaluable in launching the project and recruiting a diverse group of thirty research participants from thirteen different countries of origin. Despite team members' immigrant roots and sensitivity to immigration-related issues, the team was ultimately composed of U.S. citizens and residents with much more secure status than our research participants. As white citizen women, Christina and Alaska also did not experience being targeted by the racialized anti-immigrant attacks that proliferated once Trump took office that impacted other research team and CAB members. As the convener of the research team and CAB, Christina occupied a position of power relative to the students, though as described later, the hierarchical nature of this relationship transformed over time. Research team members occupied positions of relative privilege and reflected on this regularly during our team meetings as we sought to adopt a collective posture of humility and solidarity (Bejarano et al. 2019).

Scholarship on undocumented youth foregrounds the importance of creating and occupying safe spaces, particularly in response to political instability (Nájera 2020; Nuñez Janes, Ovalle, and Plancarte 2018). While college campuses and community-based organizations (CBOs) serve as critical safe spaces for immigrant young adults, our initial research in 2016 revealed that most participants were not actively engaged in these spaces. A few had participated in youth programming and/or filed initial DACA applications at Latinx immigrant-serving CBOs, but the majority had not. Some noted that these types of CBOs simply did not exist for their ethnic communities; although the D.C. metropolitan region is a hyperdiverse immigrant gateway, many national-origin groups do not live in discernable enclaves and are instead dispersed throughout the region (Singer 2012). Most of our research participants were also not active in groups on their community college or university campuses; as largely commuter students who worked (in some cases, multiple) off-campus jobs, they were not deeply enmeshed in campus life. A handful of participants shared that they really did not know other DACA recipients and were curious about how their experiences compared to others who had participated in our project.

As an initial step in trying to facilitate connections, we held a community meeting to present findings in March 2017. During the meeting, some participants expressed a desire to become more involved in the research in an ongoing way, particularly given the distress they were experiencing during Trump's early months in office. Although Maryland has historically been an immigrant-friendly state, the notable uptick in federal enforcement actions was evoking new fears in local immigrant communities less accustomed to them (Getrich and Ortez-Rivera 2018). We brainstormed about what form that might take, ultimately deciding to create our own space and way of holding space in the form of a CAB; importantly, our CAB was an entity that was not embedded within any institution (Duncan 2018), as our members were not all affiliated with any one university or CBO.

We purposefully invited individuals who came from different countries of origin; represented different ages, life course phases, genders, sexualities, and religious backgrounds; spanned from full-time college students to nonstudent/full-time (plus) employees; and lived in different jurisdictions within the D.C. metropolitan region. Given the diverse sample from phase I, it was important to us to seek representation and forge connections across multiple axes of identity. We invited eight individuals to join the CAB, all of whom accepted. In this chapter, we refer to members by the pseudonyms Angélica, Annisa, Brandon, Elena, Madeline, Nayeli, Pau, and Rebeca.

As we launched the CAB, we sought to accompany our eight CAB members by fostering sociality. We spent a good amount of time initially establishing relationships and building community, which was especially important given the weight of the DACA rescission news that framed the meeting. Most participants did not know each other, though some unexpected connections immediately emerged. Angélica and Annisa realized that they knew each other from a uniquely DACA-related situation: both participated in a summer research program but had encountered a snafu in getting paid when they were improperly classified as international students. They deduced that they were in the same situation due to their DACA status. They were glad to quickly encounter a familiar face, albeit in a very different—and more affirmative—context. Another pair (Nayeli and Elena) knew each other because they were both in the same cohort of a scholarship program that supports first-generation and low-income students focused on entrepreneurship and community development. Unlike many other scholarship programs, DACA recipients are explicitly eligible for this program. Research team members also knew new CAB members through their personal networks, which also facilitated connection and comfort. Ana and Brandon knew each other through a family member of Ana's who had worked with him at a local clinic, and Alaska and Rebecca had been co-workers in a physical rehabilitation center, and subsequently became friends.

By the end of the meeting, we brainstormed about what we would call the group, settling on the DACA-mented DREAM Team. The group felt strongly about foregrounding being DACA recipients since visibility surrounding DACA was crucial as it was under attack; they also were drawn to the affirmative messaging relating to dreams. We also set our agenda for the year ahead, which was focused on charting local health-based resources, designing interview guides for health care providers serving immigrant young adults, and grappling with the emerging and ongoing mental health needs of DACA recipients. We also decided that meeting twice a year would be a good frequency given everyone's increasingly busy schedules.

Reflecting back on the CAB's formation, we knew that we would need to focus on building meaning and purpose into our relationships as part of forging sociality and be malleable to attend to ever-evolving developments related to DACA (Long and Moore 2012, 41). It also became clear after the first meeting that the CAB meetings themselves could serve as a resource through which those in the know (like Pau) were able to share these developments with others in a supportive space where they could process the information in community. While some members expressed an initial concern that they were not "experts," we communicated that, indeed, they were in this space, and that their knowledge and insights were critical. We did our best to ensure that the meeting tone was more informal, despite the fact that we distributed agendas ahead of time (which some members more accustomed to workplace culture had requested).

In July 2019 (during our fifth meeting), members completed an evaluation assessing how the CAB had served them, benefits they had experienced, challenges in participating, potential future research directions, and additional roles they would like to see the CAB serve. The comments highlighted clearly that the CAB had, indeed, been a "safe space to share personal thoughts with others who are experiencing the same" and "a great outlet for sharing experiences," as members commented. As our CAB solidified, it became a space for members to connect more deeply. Another member noted that a benefit of the CAB had been "listening to others' stories so I don't feel alone. It has given me a voice to help those who have or are going through the same struggles." Thus, it also became clear that accompanying and helping each other through these struggles was a critically important function of the CAB.

Accompaniment as Forging Solidarity and Sharing Navigational Capital (2018–early 2020)

Continuing forward into 2018, we transformed our mode of accompaniment more concertedly into the realm of solidarity. We always started our meetings with updates as we became more invested in developments that transpired in our lives. As one member reflected in the evaluation, "I enjoy the company of the team. I get excited to hear updates from everyone's lives!" In the interim between our first and second meetings, Madeline had graduated from college, while Rebecca began a graduate program in social work (while continuing to hold down two jobs). More graduations followed in 2018 (Annisa and Pau) and 2019 (Ana, Elena, and Nayeli), and members began new postgraduation jobs in their chosen fields. We celebrated these accomplishments, though members also regularly discussed the challenges of "adulting" as DACA recipients. For instance, we lamented alongside Madeline that she was not able to put her degree in political science to use in the way she had envisioned given that her status rendered her ineligible to work in the federal government and related sectors common in the region; other members shared their experiences in missing out on other opportunities in an effort to ease her disappointment. We also applauded other hard-fought victories like Annisa's quest to get a driver's license and liberate herself from her outrageously long and convoluted bus commute (which unfolded over several meetings).

We also started learning much more about members' family members and inquiring about them as part of our broader check-ins. When Christina was eight months pregnant during the summer 2018 meeting, the CAB exuded excitement and made her promise to bring the baby to the next meeting; she obliged in January 2019 as the CAB supported her in transitioning to her new role as mother-researcher. While Christina had anxiety about this life transition potentially interrupting the flow of the CAB, CAB members signaled clearly that they intended to forge ahead and have baby Marisa join as an unofficial member. As our relationships complexified, it became clear that the boundaries of our roles as CAB members were shifting and blurring (Nuñez Janes, Ovalle, and Plancarte 2018; Unterberger 2009) as we offered support in other realms of our lives. Lopez, Kline, LeBrón, and Novak (chapter 6) similarly find that accompaniment necessarily involves sharing all aspects of our identities and lives as we prioritize forging genuine social relationships over mere research relationships.

In addition to these life transitions, relationships deepened as the Trump administration announced new executive orders and rule changes.

In fact, it just so happened that our CAB meetings often took place right alongside these late-breaking developments. While we certainly did not plan for this phenomenon, we had an already-established social support structure in place to help members process these changes. For instance, our January 2018 meeting took place a few days after the Supreme Court announced that it would hear challenges to the Muslim ban executive order; our CAB provided support as our Muslim members expressed how painful being targeted religiously compounded with the vulnerability they already felt with their precarious DACA status.

In January 2019, our meeting took place during the middle of the longest government shutdown in U.S. history. CAB members expressed their outrage at being used as political pawns, which members felt particularly acutely given all of the government employees in the D.C. region. Indeed, Rebeca's sister (a government contractor) was forced into silence as her co-workers directed their blame to DACA recipients as the source of their lost income. Stemming from our meeting, we channeled our frustrations into a collaboratively written article (Burdette et al. 2019). As we collectively processed these developments, the CAB cultivated important forms of relatedness and accordingly were able to provide nonjudgmental care (Duncan 2018). At times, our meetings felt more like a support group than a research meeting. In the evaluation, members expressed that the CAB "was an important place to express our emotions" and that "the team makes me feel important with just my presence." Given the ongoing immigration-related assaults transpiring under Trump, we were heartened that the CAB functioned effectively as a space of vulnerability and support.

Over time, and as more members pursued careers, the CAB also became a space for emerging professionals to share navigational capital related to health, education, and legal resources (Getrich et al. 2022). Alaska, Ana, and Delmis had wrapped up their undergraduate degrees and became valued members of this solidarity network; their deep investment in the CAB meant that they continued participating long after their roles as student-researchers ended. Five members of the CAB (Alaska, Angélica, Annisa, Brandon, and Rebeca) worked within health care and social services; in addition to being key players in mapping out sites of care for the project, they also shared resources with fellow CAB members for themselves and their family members, including practical tips for accessing heavily impacted community-health clinics. Three CAB members (Ana, Angélica, and Delmis) worked as advocates within school systems or educational nonprofits; Delmis and Angélica started working within the same county school system and regularly saw each other in their professional roles. Delmis also worked at an immigrant-rights organization, allowing her to not only provide regular updates on DACA but also help Annisa obtain legal guidance about the implications of her move to Virginia for her DACA renewal. In contrast to the top-down nature of "helping," these exchanges underscored the horizontal quality of solidarity, through which relations of mutuality were forged (Bellilno and Loucky 2017, 229).

During our final pre-pandemic meeting in January 2020, we talked about wanting to meet more regularly, given that the space had been so conducive to processing challenges and sharing resources. The space we had created had become a useful entity beyond its initial research purpose, and the ways we accompanied each other within it complexified. Beyond that, quite simply, we wanted to see each other more, as we relished in being able to accompany each other through life transitions. The evaluation reflected this desire, as members requested "more meetings!" and sharing "life updates with everyone in between meetings through email." Despite these affirmative aspirations, we felt slightly challenged about how exactly to actualize it, as increasingly, members had work schedule conflicts, longer commutes (a notorious facet of D.C. life), and other family responsibilities that made physically attending the meeting challenging. What we did not know at that point, of course, was that we were all about to enter into a global pandemic that would make frequent, in-person meetings an impossibility anyway.

Accompaniment as Reconfiguring Sociality and Providing Moral Support (2020–present)

As we shifted yet again into the CAB's next chapter, accompaniment took the form of reconfiguring sociality and providing moral support during the pandemic. Nuñez-Janes and Heiman (chapter 2) likewise underscore the critical importance of social support for immigrant young adults during times of crisis. Given that we had just discussed meeting more frequently, we were fairly well positioned to transition our meeting format to a virtual platform, which we started experimenting with (leveraging Ana's tech skills) in February 2020 as the pandemic spread. The trial run went well, so we established a standing day/time slot for each month. Yet it was more than just our meeting format that was changing; indeed, as with everyone, we necessarily had to reconfigure sociality in alignment with our new "lockdown lives" (van Breen et al. 2021). We also were simultaneously transforming into a new mode of research—"lockdown anthropology" of newly emerging social worlds (Long 2020a).

One of our early exercises in transforming our CAB space and reconfiguring how we engaged with each other was to generate a monthly prompt and have each member populate a shared Google document with a meme or GIF that captured our response. We started with lighter topics like, "What would you do with an extra day?" in February with members talking about extra sleep, tidying up, and trying new recipes. Our March spring-focused prompt, "What's blossoming in your life right now?" started exhibiting some of the larger malaise that was enveloping us as members brought up mental and physical health, the need for self-care, staying sane amid the chaos, and finding creativity. By April, we were squarely grappling with the gravity of the pandemic as we answered, "What do you look forward to doing once again when life returns to normal?" (Unbeknownst to us at the time, we were still months if not years away from life returning to any kind of "normal.") Our responses reflected our intense need for connection, as we talked about missing giving people hugs, being able to see crazy/funny co-workers in person, and going to concerts and bars with friends.

We also started using the space to forge new configurations of care that did not require physical co-presence (Long 2020b, 250). Some members confronted COVID every day in their jobs as a paramedic (Alaska), mental health provider in a health care system (Annisa), and information specialist in a major public transportation system (Madeline). They gave us important updates about how things really were out in the world and how their workplaces were (or were not) managing the pandemic. We, in turn, provided them support in confronting illness, death, and the heavy weight of their work. Alaska's job during this time was especially intense, as she and her fellow paramedics had to follow challenging protocols about who to leave behind in the interest of containing the virus and preserving limited resources. Though their schedules were irregular, they still managed to join us, even calling in from their phone in the car. As front-line workers, they were early vaccine recipients when it became available, and shared their experiences with us, including the side effects (less well known initially) and, eventually, prized information about vaccine availability.

Those of us who had the "pandemic privilege" (Horton 2021) of working remotely were grappling with a different set of challenges: disruption to our normal workday routines and social isolation. Indeed, "social distancing" was deeply impacting our relationships and challenging our capacity to provide more normative forms of care (Long 2020b). Christina struggled considerably initially with remote teaching with her one-year-old at home while also caring for multiple family members with (non-COVID) illnesses and challenging circumstances exacerbated by the pandemic. The CAB meetings became a lifeline, offering a brief but regular respite from work and caregiving responsibilities and a dose of therapeutic connection. We did some of what other groups of people were doing at the time: shared streaming show recommendations, exchanged grocery shopping strategies, laughed when family members crashed our carefully curated Zoom spaces, and cooed over new pandemic pets (like Madeline's bunny). Early on in the pandemic, a member got COVID and became a long-COVID patient. Our gatherings were one of the few social outlets she had, and this was one of the ways that we were able to show up for her. We were heartened to see her improvement over time as she shared that resuming kickboxing was one of the things she most looked forward to when life returned to normal.

By summer 2020, some members became involved in providing direct support to more vulnerable community members. Delmis's CBO launched a food drive to distribute necessities to immigrant families ineligible for support from the federal government. She distributed packages and shared information about how we could get involved (even if we could not be there in person alongside her). Pau, who had already spearheaded a number of different initiatives (like a scholarship program for undocumented youth) grew concerned that the most vulnerable immigrants were still being left out of these organizational efforts given the high demand for services and limited resources. She and three of her friends created a crowdfunding campaign for emergency funds for immigrants. When the first coronavirus economic impact payments went out, their campaign encouraged people to donate some of their payment if their employment had not been disrupted. We already had a good solidarity network in place for disseminating information about these emerging initiatives in support of the immigrant community. For some members who had health conditions or vulnerable family members that precluded them from being more directly involved (like Christina), these were concrete actions they could take.

During this period of time, our priorities shifted considerably. Though we continued to share resources, process the latest DACA developments (like the Supreme Court's decision to overturn the Trump administration's rescission of DACA in July 2020), and brainstorm new research directions (as we began our third phase of research in August 2020), the CAB was much more about accompanying each other through the pandemic and providing each other the forms of pandemic moral support each of us needed, which varied depending on our individual circumstances. The CAB became a virtual "third place" for cultivating connectedness during a time in which we experienced disconnection from our regular relationships and ways of engaging socially (Butler and Diaz 2016; Hardy 2020). Indeed, the CAB served as an innovative mode of "corona sociality" (Long 2020b, 248) through which we cultivated evolving forms of care and support for each other. This moral engagement and togetherness unquestionably became the most defining feature of the CAB in its pandemic chapter.

Conclusion

In its five years of existence, the DACA-mented DREAM Team has unquestionably served its intended research purpose—we mapped local health care sites, formulated interview questions, collectively reviewed numerous interpretive reports, and coauthored a research article. The CAB made an indelible imprint on the directions the research moved during a very turbulent period for DACA recipients and the immigrant communities in which they are embedded. Indeed, our collective efforts have enabled us to forge an effective partnership (in multiple senses) that intertwines research, practice, and care work. Though there is a long tradition of critically engaged anthropologists collaborating with existing immigrant-rights organizations and activists to actualize their collective social justice agendas, our CAB demonstrates the value of creating longer term partnerships with those who are not conventionally active in these spaces.

Our CAB has also transformed and served in ways we certainly did not envision when we formed it. Through these shifts, we have accompanied each other in a range of different ways, underscoring how accompaniment is, indeed, a multivalent mode of practice. Initially, accompaniment meant creating space and fostering sociality among DACA recipients who were not active in immigration-focused CBOs or campus groups and largely did not know many others with the same status. Over time, accompaniment transformed into horizontal solidarity through which members leveraged professional connections and shared their navigational capital in advocating for immigrant communities. The connections we forged also made participation much more meaningful and blurred our roles as we accompanied each other through successes, challenges, and major life transitions.

As the pandemic hit, accompanying each other meant fundamentally reconfiguring the ways we interacted with each other to buffer some of the social isolation and malaise that members were experiencing. This shift underscored that research itself can take on the form of care and investment in human relationships (Saxton 2021, 24). In the initial months of the pandemic, the CAB was an important outlet for us to accompany each other through great uncertainty and abrupt changes to our everyday lives. Through it, we forged a different kind of intimacy in our relationships with each other that was rooted in our common humanity. Indeed, as Saxton (2021, 23) notes, this type of relationship building—forged on a foundation of trust and shared commitments to effecting social change—can itself constitute a form of activism. Indeed, we see these quieter forms of everyday activism as being complementary to more overt and traditional modalities of political engagement (Getrich 2021). We also believe that this deep relationship building may also serve as the foundation for more conventional forms of advocacy and longer term partnerships that can pivot to adapt to the broader sociopolitical context.

Despite our affirmative experiences with our adaptable and responsive CAB, we have started encountering some difficulties in convening it, underscoring that despite its plasticity, accompaniment can be difficult to sustain over time. One challenge we have increasingly faced is scheduling, given that many of our members have numerous responsibilities and obligations that they did not when they were younger. Many of them work in jobs that do not have eight-to-five workday schedules; especially for members who work in health care and education, evenings (when we have traditionally met) are challenging. Some members have also changed jobs and even moved into different states and time zones, further complicating their participation. As we transitioned to a virtual format, we eventually contended with significant Zoom fatigue. While there was some novelty to our initial pandemic CAB meetings, as we settled into pandemic life a few months later, many of us were simply too Zoomed out to think about calling in to one more meeting, even if it was a space of social support. While we have held regular meetings at our usual meeting intervals, participation started dwindling into 2021.

But yet, the CAB continues to hold a special place for each of us. When we have reached out to CAB members individually about research activities, they are immediately responsive and always inquire about how everyone is doing. When CAB members encounter each other socially or in the context of work, they continue to express their enthusiasm about the CAB and their apologies for not being as active as they were previously. Many times, CAB members reach out to Christina just to check in, provide an update, or schedule a catch-up call. Thus, even if we are not actively co-present at CAB "meetings" (a term we certainly use more loosely at this point), the relationships endure and can quickly be activated; this suggests to us that accompaniment can and may take on new forms outside of our group structure and into the future. The relationships of trust, concern, and care have transformed as the "space" of the CAB has moved away from physical co-presence and formal structure and more into the realm of the relational and informal. The heart of the CAB and its enduring legacy nearly five years later is indeed the multifaceted relationships we forged as we have accompanied each other through incredibly challenging times in all of our lives.

References

Bejarano, Carolina Alonso, Lucia López Juárez, Mirian Mijangos García, and Daniel Goldstein. 2019. *Decolonizing Ethnography: Undocumented Immigrants and New Directions in Social Science.* Durham, NC: Duke University Press.

Bellino, Michelle J., and James Loucky. 2017. "Education as Solidarity." *Anthropology and Education Quarterly* 48 (3): 229–232.

Burdette, Alaska, Elizabeth Chavez, Mai Diouf, Christina M. Getrich, Dania Leiva, Katterin Leiva, and Ana Ortez-Rivera. 2019. "The DACA-Mented DREAM Team: Guiding Research and Building Social Support amidst Immigration-Related Uncertainty." *Practicing Anthropology* 41 (2): 8–16.

Butler, Stuart M., and Carmen Diaz. 2016. "'Third Places' as Community Builders." The Brookings Institute. https://www.brookings.edu/blog/up-front/2016/09/14/third-places-as-community-builders/.

Duncan, Whitney L. 2018. "Acompañamiento / Accompaniment." Society for Cultural Anthropology, January 31, 2018. https://culanth.org/fieldsights/acompa%C3%B1amiento-accompaniment.

Getrich, Christina M. 2021. "'People Show Up in Different Ways': DACA Recipients' Everyday Activism in a Time of Heightened Immigration-Related Insecurity." *Human Organization* 80 (1): 27–36.

Getrich, Christina M., and Ana Ortez-Rivera. 2018. "ICE Was Like an Urban Legend Here in Maryland." Society for Cultural Anthropology, January 31, 2018. https://culanth.org/fieldsights/ice-was-like-an-urban-legend-here-in-maryland.

Getrich, Christina M., Ana Ortez-Rivera, Delmis Umanzor, and Alaska Burdette. 2022. "Manoeuvering through the Multilayered Jurisdictional Policy Patchwork: DACA Recipients' Navigational Capital in the Washington, D.C. Metropolitan Region." *Ethnic and Racial Studies* 46 (1): 141–165.

Hacker, Karen. 2017. *Community-Based Participatory Research*. Thousand Oaks, CA: SAGE Publications.

Hardy, Lisa J. 2020. "Negotiating Inequality: Disruption and COVID-19 in the United States." *City and Society* 32 (2): 1–9.

Horton, Sarah. 2021. "On Pandemic Privilege: Reflections on a 'Home-Bound Pandemic Ethnography.'" *Journal for the Anthropology of North America* 24 (2): 98–107.

Israel, Barbara A., Eugenia Eng, Amy J. Schulz, Edith A. Parker, and David Satcher. 2005. *Methods in Community-Based Participatory Research for Health*. San Francisco, CA: Jossey Bass.

Long, Nicholas J. 2020a. "Lockdown Anthropology and Online Surveys: Unprecedented Methods for Unprecedented Times." *Studies in Indian Politics* 8 (2): 294–297.

Long, Nicholas J. 2020b. "From Social Distancing to Social Containment: Reimagining Sociality for the Coronavirus Pandemic." *Medicine Anthropology Theory* 7 (2): 247–260.

Long, Nicholas J., and Henrietta L. Moore. 2012. "Sociality Revisited: Setting a New Agenda." *Cambridge Anthropology* 30 (1): 40–47.

Miller, Alisa B., Osob M. Issa, Emily Hahn, Naima Y. Agalab, and Saida M. Abdi. 2021. "Developing Advisory Boards within Community-Based Participatory Approaches to Improve Mental Health among Refugee Communities." *Progress in Community Health Partnerships: Research, Education, and Action* 15 (1): 107–116.

Nájera, Jennifer R. 2020. "Creating Safe Space for Undocumented Students: Building on Politically Unstable Ground." *Anthropology and Educational Quarterly* 51 (3): 341–358.

Newman, Susan D., Jeannette O. Andrews, Gayenell S. Magwood, Carolyn Jenkins, Melissa J. Cox, and Deborah C. Williamson. 2011. "Community Advisory Boards in Community-Based Participatory Research: A Synthesis of Best Processes." *Preventing Chronic Disease* 8 (3): A70.

Nuñez-Janes, Mariela, Mario Ovalle, and Stephanie Plancarte. 2018. "Creating Sanctuary: Practices of Acompañamiento." Society for Cultural Anthropology, January 31, 2018. https://culanth.org/fieldsights/creating-sanctuary-practices-of-acompa%C3%B1amiento.

Ortega, Sigolène, Megan Stamey McAlvain, Katherine J. Briant, Sarah Hohl, and Beti Thompson. 2018. "Perspectives of Community Advisory Board Members in a Community-Academic Partnership." *Journal of Health Care for the Poor and Underserved* 29 (4): 1529–1543.

Raymond-Flesh, Marissa, Rachel Siemons, Nadereh Pourat, Ken Jacobs, and Claire D. Brindis. 2014. "'There is No Help Out There and If There Is, It's Really Hard to Find': A Qualitative Study of the Health Concerns and Health Care Access of Latino 'DREAMers.'" *Journal of Adolescent Health* 55 (3): 323–328.

Rustage, Kieran, Alison Crawshaw, Saliha Majeed-Hajaj, Anna Deal, Laura Nellums, Yusuf Ciftci, Sebastian S. Fuller, Lucy Goldsmith, Jon S. Friedlan, and Sally Hargreaves. 2021. "Participatory Approaches in the Development of Health Interventions for Migrants: A Systematic Review." *BMJ Open* 11 (1): e053678.

Santiago Martinez, Pedro, Claudia Muñoz, Mariela Nuñez-Janes, Stephen Pavey, Fidel Castro Rodriguez, and Marco Saavedra. 2020. *Eclipse of Dreams: The Undocumented-Led Struggle for Freedom*. Chico, CA: AK Press.

Saxton, Dvera I. 2021. *The Devil's Fruit: Farmworkers, Health, and Environmental Justice*. New Brunswick, NJ: Rutgers University Press.

Singer, Audrey. 2012. "Metropolitan Washington: A New Immigrant Gateway." In *Hispanic Migration and Urban Development: Studies from Washington, D.C.*, edited by Enrique Pumar, 1–32. Bingley, UK: Emerald Publishing Group.

Stacciarini, Jeanne-Marie R., Rebekah Felicia Smith, Brenda Wiens, Awilda Pérez, Barbara Locke, and Melody LaFlam. 2015. "'I Didn't Ask to Come to this Country . . . I Was a Child': The Mental Health Implications of Growing Up Undocumented." *Journal of Immigrant and Minority Health* 17:1225–1230.

Sudhinaraset, May, Irving Ling, Tu My To, Jason Melo, and Thu Quach. 2017a. "Dreams Deferred: Contextualizing the Health and Psychosocial Needs of Undocumented Asian and Pacific Islander Young Adults in Northern California." *Social Science and Medicine* 184:144–152.

Sudhinaraset, May, Tu My To, Irving Ling, Jason Melo, and Josue Chavarin. 2017b. "The Influence of Deferred Action for Childhood Arrivals on Undocumented

Asian and Pacific Islander Young Adults: Through a Social Determinants of Health Lens." *Journal of Adolescent Health* 60 (6): 741–746.

Unterberger, Alayne. 2009. "The Blur: Balancing Applied Anthropology, Activism, and Self vis-à-vis Immigrant Communities." *NAPA Bulletin* 31:1–12.

Van Breen, Jolien A., Maja Kutlaca, Yasin Koç, Bertus F. Jeronimus, Anne Margit Reitsema, Veljko Jovanović, Maximilian Agostini et al. 2021. "Lockdown Lives: A Longitudinal Study of Inter-Relationships among Feelings of Loneliness, Social Contacts, and Solidarity during the COVID-19 Lockdown in Early 2020." *Personality and Social Psychology Bulletin* 48 (9): 1315–1330.

Wallerstein, Nina, and Bonnie Duran. 2006. "Using Community-Based Participatory Research to Address Health Disparities." *Health Promotion and Practice* 7:312–323.

Wallerstein, Nina, Bonnie Duran, John Oetzel, and Meredith Minkler. 2017. *Community-Based Participatory Research for Health: Advancing Social and Health Equity*, 3rd ed. San Francisco: Jossey-Bass.

CHAPTER 2

Acompañamiento as a Critical Pedagogy in Action

MARIELA NUÑEZ-JANES AND DAN HEIMAN

The first meeting of what became the Bilingual Homework Hotline (BHH) took place on April 30, 2020, while the Denton ISD (DISD) school district in Texas, like others around the country, moved all of its instructional activities online in response to the COVID-19 pandemic. As Denton residents and professors engaged in our community, we knew that our schools were struggling, so we asked, How can we help? Twelve individuals including professors from the University of North Texas (UNT), Texas Woman's University (TWU), along with staff from the district's Dual Language and English as a Second Language Department (DL/ESL), and G.O.A.L. (Guys and Girls Operating as Leaders after-school soccer and leadership program) gathered virtually over Zoom to discuss how we could leverage our expertise and resources to support Latinx students and families. During the first of what became ongoing weekly virtual meetings we found out that eight hundred students from DISD were unaccounted for. Most of them were from school zones within the district with large percentages of Latinx students and 210 of them were bilingual. Our weekly virtual meetings crystallized into the organizing of a homework hotline modeled after the parent hotline established by the district's DL/ESL department.

Since the fall of 2020, when the BHH was launched, hundreds of "homework helpers" from an applied anthropology program and pre-service bilingual teacher courses have helped emergent bilingual students with their homework by answering thousands of phone calls. The demand for the BHH homework hotline has steadily increased even as DISD returned to in-person classes. During the end of its second year, before the 2022 spring semester was over, the BHH received over a thousand calls from emergent bilingual students, more than any other semester. Emergent bilingual students from grades three through eight call to get help with their math, reading, and science homework. We quickly realized that students were calling the BHH for other reasons. Emergent bilingual students sometimes call just to have a "homework helper" be with them or accompany them as they do their homework. For one emergent bilingual student who was attending school remotely, having a "homework helper" listen to her while she read in a Zoom breakout room made her feel like she was at school. To not feel alone, *no sentirse solo,* despite the isolating context of the pandemic is an important way in which the BHH is about more than homework. We call this space *acompañamiento* and draw on the work of educational ethnographers and theorists in conceptualizing it as a "pluridimensional pedagogy" (Planella 2008) practiced through "empathetic fusion" (Sepúlveda 2011) that "risks an act of love" (Freire 2000).

We were inspired and guided by the work of feminist (Villenas 2019), action (Stringer and Aragón 2021), and critical scholars (Freire 2000) who challenged us to side with those in the margins by aiming to engage in non-exploitative practices (Bejarano et al. 2019; Fernandes 2003; San Pedro 2021) during a time of great urgency. We were driven by our interest to put our knowledge and skills to use for the benefit of the Latinx community. This problem-centered approach prioritizes peoples' struggles. We rely on this stance to lead our inquiry in the BHH as we try to center the struggles of our Latinx community. We call this approach to ethnographic inquiry being "*críticos no criticones*" (Nuñez-Janes and Heiman 2021). In our context as academics and particularly during the pandemic and as a result of the uprisings led and inspired by the Black Lives Matter movement we saw many calls for research about the challenges experienced by Latinx and BIPOC communities. However, we felt frustrated by extractive research agendas that pursue knowledge without necessarily connecting it to action and local change during a time of great need. Drawing on Charles Hale's (2006) distinction between activist anthropology and cultural critique, we call critical approaches that stop short of taking action a *criticón* approach, where research is conducted for the sake of knowledge, and circumstances of despair are critiqued, maybe recommendations for changes are made, but no attempt is made to create change (Heiman et al. forthcoming). We differentiate this from an activist/*crítico* stance where critical understandings and critiques are made and used as a foundation to take action and make changes.

In this chapter we reflect on the years since the BHH has been serving emergent bilinguals in Denton. We draw on our experiences, extensive note taking, and record keeping to trace the contours of acompañamiento as a critical pedagogical and ethnographic practice reflecting on our engagement with the BHH as we attempted to be "críticos no criticones." In particular, we ask, What does acompañamiento look like in the BHH? What does it involve? Our engagement with the BHH is teaching us that acompañamiento is a practice of critical consciousness that involves taking action by: putting Latinx families at the center of inquiry instead of prioritizing research or academic outcomes (putting people, not research, first), engaging in constant reflection that informs and is informed by taking action, unlearning the stigma of illegality by centering lived experiences, and creating new visions that forge paths toward collective freedom and liberation.

As professors and educational ethnographers, we are positioned in this space as fully human. Mariela, also known as *profe*, is a 1.5-generation immigrant Latina born in Maracaibo, Venezuela, with family ties that bind her to Puerto Rico, where her *mami* was born and raised. Mariela migrated to the United States in 1983, where she reunited with her older brother and sister who were attending college. She was followed by her parents who migrated later. She attended a school in Minnesota, where she was one of a handful of students of color and learned English through the sink-or-swim approach. It was at this time that she received a letter of removal from Immigration and Naturalization Services (INS) before it became ICE. The pain caused by the threat of forced family separation and language assimilation inspire her research and teaching. Mariela dedicates her career to trying to undo the hurt of U.S. schooling through local research, advocacy, and mentoring that focuses on recovering the cultural assets of Latinx youth and their families. She has lived in Denton for nineteen years, where, in addition to being a professor, she advocates and organizes with the immigrant community.

Dan is a white cisgender male with more than twenty years in bilingual education in the United States and Mexico as a classroom teacher, teacher educator, and researcher whose work focuses on justice-oriented processes in dual-language bilingual education (DLBE) contexts and the preparation of future *maestrxs bilingües* for those same contexts. He actively strives to leverage his bilingualism to challenge raciolinguistic ideologies and other deficit-driven processes that marginalize racialized bilinguals. In *comunidad* with other critical scholars in DLBE, Dan has proposed and documented the enactment of critical consciousness at the policy, classroom, and community levels to highlight the urgency of countering DLBE gentrification and transforming conceptualizations of academic achievement, bilingualism/biliteracy, and sociocultural competence (Dorner et al. 2023; Heiman et al. 2024).

In Denton, the pandemic made Latinx immigrant families more vulnerable. Immigrants in Texas were doubly impacted by Trump's zero-tolerance policies and Governor Abbott's anti-immigrant attacks. Laws like SB4, requiring law enforcement to inquire about immigration status during routine stops, and the Texas attorney general's lawsuits challenging DACA created an uncertain climate for Denton's immigrants. The fear of an unknown disease was further driving the Latinx community into the shadows. Families were afraid of seeking medical attention and were also afraid to get help from local aid groups and nonprofits because of language barriers and/or because they often required driver's licenses, which are unavailable to undocumented immigrants in Texas. During our weekly meetings we found out that some families were choosing to return to Mexico.

La Linea de Tareas

The BHH rolled out on September 14, 2020, five months after our first meeting. This first iteration of the BHH helped lay the foundation for how the hotline operates today. University students or homework helpers participate in a training webinar where we explain how the hotline works, share DISD's requirements, and provide resources to help during the helpers' sessions with DISD students. This also includes explaining DISD's required volunteer background check and coming up with strategies for university students who don't have a social security number.

During the fall of 2020, the BHH operated from 4 to 8 p.m., Monday through Thursday, serving grades three through eight. Students left a voicemail with their name, callback number, and subject they needed help with. The voicemail would be retrieved by a university student leader who would call the student back and share a Zoom link where they would join a homework helper. Along with our college students we participated as leaders and homework helpers and reflected on the week's activities during our weekly meetings and through the assignments we created for students in our classes.

Resulting from these reflections were adaptations in our use of technology, like using breakout rooms to facilitate emergent bilinguals' and homework helpers' engagement during the BHH sessions. We encouraged homework helpers to work in pairs, especially in cases where there was a mismatch between the linguistic preferences of emergent bilinguals and university student volunteers. In addition, we asked homework helpers to use the time when they waited for calls to talk to one another about strategies to engage and support emergent bilinguals who called the BHH. During the first semester this was critical as emergent bilinguals and families in DISD were learning about the BHH. There were days when we did not receive calls or when homework helpers spent their time without helping students. This was particularly disappointing for university students who were eager to help. During this time, we began encouraging homework helpers to lean into discomfort as a way to navigate challenges and to turn instances that seemed paralyzing and unproductive into opportunities for creative engagement. In the spring of 2021, the BHH began integrating appointments with students who wanted help during a specific time or in a particular subject. We also added an 11 a.m.–1 p.m. time slot, with a middle school classroom providing the opportunity for "homework helpers" to access an in-person classroom via Zoom when schools fully reopened.

Creating New Visions, Forging Paths Toward Freedom

Acompañamiento in the BHH is experienced through the prioritizing of relationship building. It took us months of talking and listening to DISD representatives, community members, and colleagues to come up with the BHH as one way to address our initial question of how we can help.

To us the BHH hotline feels transformational and liberatory because we are constantly taking action and engaging a critical stance as we center relational community values like *confianza*/trust and *comunidad*/community. We don't claim that the BHH is the answer to liberation or that it is a space without challenges or contradictions. We are, however, certain that as we are urged to return to how things were before the pandemic, refusing normalcy allows us to maintain and nurture the relational space we created in the BHH. We are inspired by the growing number of students calling the hotline and the continuous innovations to engage in the Zoom space.

Constant Reflection that Informs and Is Informed by Taking Action

We are critical of the circumstances affecting the Latinx families involved in the BHH, we are critical of the district and our own institutions' approaches to research and to the pandemic, and we are also critical of our own approaches. Yet, we engage in self-reflection to intervene purposefully and strategically to make change. Relying on the funds of knowledge of Latinx communities is part of this purposeful approach. Specifically, *confianza*/trust through the practice of critical listening is instrumental to the collaboration across institutions and to building relationships with emergent bilingual students and families while using technology. Emphasizing relationships and relationship building, particularly across institutional divides, allows us to disrupt some of the power imbalances between administrators, faculty, and teachers and to center the funds of knowledge of Latinx communities as assets instead of deficits.

Critical listening led to an interrogation of the curriculum and the needs of emergent bilinguals, which led to action (Nuñez-Janes and Heiman 2021). While critical listening is a crucial action, it also generates a praxis-cycle in which knowledge is generated from experiences while experiences are also legitimized. In the BHH emergent bilingual students and university homework helpers accompany each other in this cycle. For example, as we learned more about the needs of students, the 11 a.m.–1 p.m. time slot was modified to include the Spanish version of *The Seven Habits of Highly Effective Teens* (Covey 2014) into the curriculum. The DL/ESL program was reading this text with parents as part of their virtual weekly Spanish book club. The book choice generated tensions and opportunities to take action with the *7 Habits*. We critically listened to the interactions that were taking place around the *7 Habits* and noticed that emergent bilingual students had a hard time making sense of the book, not because they did not understand it but because it did not reflect their experiences. These students were already struggling in school and were largely recent arrivals or first-generation immigrants.

We started making adjustments in our use of the *7 Habits* by incorporating multicultural texts (España and Herrera 2020; Espinoza and Ascenzi-Moreno 2021), videos, and recorded *testimonios* from university students about their journeys to college. We opened up the opportunity to listen more deeply to emergent bilingual students by working with them on a vision board where they could voice their goals and aspirations. These adjustments allowed us to take action by reconfiguring the knowledge that informed the habits and connecting them to the epistemologies and experiences of immigrant emergent bilinguals (Fregoso Bailón and De Lissovoy 2019; Sánchez and García 2022). Emergent bilingual students and university homework helpers were able to engage in intercultural exchanges rooted in real-life experiences with the habits. This included translanguaging and legitimizing goals and aspirations beyond college.

The necessity to take action also leads us to engage in transgressions by working across disciplinary, institutional, and epistemological borders. Our weekly meetings are composed of professors, graduate students, and practitioners from various disciplines including anthropology, teacher education, and social work. Beyond these interdisciplinary conversations we transgress local borders by working across institutions. These kinds of collaborations between two local universities and a school district are unique and we are not aware of any local examples where TWU, UNT, and DISD have come together in a collaboration that centers Latinx families and spans multiple years. In addition, we transgress epistemological borders by bringing together educators, scholars, and administrators that are in relationship with Latinx communities in various ways. Some of us are Latinx ourselves and our heritage includes Mexico, Venezuela, Puerto Rico, El Salvador, and Nicaragua. Others are related to Latinx communities because of their partners or because they have an interest in the language and culture. Further, we transgress epistemological borders through the various perspectives we bring to the hotline. Particularly, these are reflected in the tensions between discourses that center the aims of the BHH as a way to bridge learning loss versus emphasizing the holistic needs of emergent bilingual students and their families. Centering the epistemologies of emergent bilinguals is more than about offering help with homework in Spanish. We thus see the BBH as transgressing instrumental aims in education through engaging in deeper and more critical ways with the *comunidad* and their needs (Dyerness and Sepúlveda 2020; Martínez et al. 2020; Nuñez-Janes and Ovalle 2016).

These transgressions are anchored in building relationships. Relationship building is done between homework helpers and emergent bilingual students, between scholars and practitioners, and between professors and college students. Part of this is accomplished by working with rather than against our individual and collective feelings. Our focus on leaning into discomfort as a pedagogical strategy for university student volunteers is also a strategy in our weekly meetings. We started the BHH with a vision but without a specific roadmap, particularly when it came to the integration of technology and the managing of hundreds of volunteers. Like and with our students, we feel frustration and anger and simultaneously experience joy and a sense of accomplishment as we participate in the BHH. The opportunity to feel forges relationships and fuels the Zoom space with personality. Feeling together helps to establish *confianza*. We began to notice that conversations around homework/academics were indeed taking place alongside discussions of identity, experiences and realities of living in a pandemic, university students sharing their journeys to college, students' love of sports and the arts, and acompañamiento. Ultimately emphasizing relationship building de-centers the university student as the dispenser of knowledge around homework and help. This de-centering of a banking approach to "homework help" (Freire 2000) creates opportunities for homework helpers to engage in praxis in conjunction with critical theoretical perspectives from their respective courses in teacher education and anthropology. The virtual medium provides an opportunity to reimagine others and in the case of the BHH hotline to see ourselves through the lens of the work that we do together, transgressing the limitations and assumptions imposed on us because of how our bodies are interpreted when we are in-person. Maybe what we do in the hotline feels bigger, transgressive, and liberatory because it is online. Regardless, the virtual space does provide opportunities to reimagine and to engage in what Gloria Ladson-Billings (2021) calls the "hard-reset" in education. Further, as bell hooks (1994) contends, education can be a "practice of freedom" when teaching aims to challenge and disrupt racism, sexism, and classism. As we work together in relationship and accompany each other, we find the path toward our collective freedom by taking action.

Unlearning

Unlearning the stigma of being immigrant and undocumented and unlearning the idea that learning is comfortable are also part of the transformational power of acompañamiento in the BHH. Incorporating *testimonios* as part of our teaching pedagogy helps us disrupt and interrogate the relation between teacher and learner—and in our case homework helper and emergent bilingual student—while allowing us to frame the experiences of Latinx and marginalized youth as academically relevant.

In the spring of 2021, we were reminded of the urgency to speak with and for immigrant communities locally as Texas experienced a snowstorm and freezing temperatures that caused failure in the electric power grid resulting in death and major damages to people's homes. Everyone involved in the BHH was affected in various ways. Locally, failure of the power grid also revealed failure of the city and well-intended groups to translate emergency information and create intake processes for resource distribution accessible to Denton residents without social security numbers or Texas driver's licenses. The invisibility and isolation of the Latinx immigrant community in Denton became apparent to some of us in the BHH as we experienced another crisis. Some of us took action informally by translating city emergency announcements and advocating on behalf of undocumented families while sharing information with the DL/ESL program staff who had direct contact with families. Information in Spanish about food distribution, warming stations, boiling water notices, and housing was lifesaving to immigrant families.

We incorporated *testimonio* in our classes because we understood that bearing witness is lifesaving and shatters stigmas. In Mariela's anthropology class, homework helpers created *testimonios* about their experiences with the high school to college transition. These were shared virtually with a group of middle school students. In their *testimonios*, college students discussed various pathways to educational success along with the challenges they confronted while navigating the educational system. All of the *testimonios* resonated with emergent bilingual students in authentic ways. In particular, Valeria's testimonio, "Immigrant Journey to College," about her experiences as an undocumented student, shattered many assumptions emergent bilingual students, their teachers, and families held about being undocumented and going to college (Martínez-Napoles 2021). The *testimonio* not only sparked conversations about what was considered a taboo topic in many local classrooms but also generated follow-up actions in the form of workshops for teachers and families.

Unlearning in the BHH also involves discomfort. In the case of putting together the *testimonios*, university students had to engage uncomfortable truths about their lives and the lives of their fellow classmates. Writing, recording, and sharing about her journey to college as an undocumented student was uncomfortable for Valeria, as it was for all the students who were asked to critically reflect about their lives as part of an anthropology class. Similarly, hearing about these multiple truths was difficult for emergent bilinguals, the teachers, and families who participated in meetings and workshops.

Education does not have to hurt. Indeed, when it comes to immigrant youth, we know that assimilationist approaches to education and zero-tolerance immigration policies hurt students, intentionally or unintentionally. What we mean by unlearning the idea that learning is comfortable is engaging the difficult realities of emergent bilingual students relationally so that youth don't feel alone in their educational journeys. As Valeria concluded in her testimonio as a last message to immigrant bilingual students, "I learned more about my world and I found out that I have important contributions to make in this world, including you." Leaning into this kind of discomfort offers opportunities to unlearn loneliness and fear.

Closing *Pensamientos* (Thoughts)

As the pandemic continues and the hotline approaches the start of its third year, it is clear to us that Texas is experiencing another crisis in the form of attacks against diversity, multicultural education, and social justice in schools. As if the debates around mask mandates in Texas were not enough, the attacks against education have further deepened with the banning of books and classroom discussions about racism and sexual orientation. In Texas, the anti–critical race theory movement is mirrored in the law approved by the governor in 2021, SB3, limiting teachers' ability to discuss issues related to diversity, inclusion, and social justice. Local subtractive efforts and whitening of school curriculums are also taking place while a federal judge issued a ruling against in-state tuition for undocumented students in a lawsuit in which UNT, where Mariela teaches, was challenged by a campus student organization, Young Conservatives of Texas (YCT). In this constant state of crisis, our focus has shifted from asking how we help to how else we can help.

We have attempted to outline what acompañamiento looks like in the BHH by reflecting on our collective practice of being *críticos no criticones* through actions that involve putting Latinx families at the center of inquiry

FIGURE 2.1 Martha Samaniego Calderón. 2019. *Translenguaje* [Painting].

instead of prioritizing research or academic outcomes, engaging in constant reflection that informs and is informed by taking action, unlearning the stigma of illegality by centering lived experiences, and creating new visions that forge paths toward collective freedom and liberation. Yet, Martha Samaniego Calderón's (2019) art, rather than our words, encapsulates best what the space of acompañamiento looks like and feels like to us. With the heart at the center as fluid tongues of color transgress shapes, spaces, and languages, acompañamiento in the BHH is *"el space de en medio, tan full of amor donde nada is separado"* (*the space in the middle, so full of love, where nothing is separate)*. Despite our best efforts, we ultimately feel that it is hard to explain what acompañamiento is and what it looks like in the BHH hotline because it is hard to disrupt the disciplining of our words, ideas, explanations, and approaches even when we push against the expectations imposed by our scholarly disciplines. We find, however, that our difficulties in articulating the significance of acompañamiento are symptomatic of anthropology's and ethnography's deep epistemological colonization. As ethnographers, we have a difficult time discussing, accounting for, and including relationships and human intimacy as integral to our scholarship and as drivers of our inquiry. We turn to Martha's artwork, a parent to DISD's bilingual students and Dan's partner, to nurture and make clearer the spaces of feeling/thinking that our disciplines prefer to maintain in the shadows or margins of our scholarship.

We closed the BHH's second year with a project during the 11 a.m.–1 p.m. time slot where students read about college, planned, and imagined their futures as they were accompanied by the book *Graciela's Dream* (Del Monte and Benavidez, 2006), a story about Graciela's journey to college. We continue to center Latinx student experiences in our courses, and we are imagining the possibility of a transborder version of the BHH to reflect the lives of students and families who are from Musquiz, Mexico, Denton's sister city. Our work with the BHH has taught us that acompañamiento requires constant commitment to ask what else we can do to help while pushing against the impetus to return to a time when the lives of Latinx immigrant youth were in the shadows of educational policies and practices. Returning to this kind of normalcy, returning to a decentering of Latinx immigrant lives in schools is not an option for us. Acompañamiento deepens our commitment to engage in educational ethnography not only for the sake of research but also with the impetus to act upon the lives of Latinx families *en convivencia* (in relationship with) those who have been on the margins for far too long.

Authors' Note: We are thankful for the contributions of our BHH *familia*: Rebeca Olvera-Alfaro, Martha Mendoza, José Robles, Teresa Luna-Taylor, Chris Ice, Mike Mattingly, César Rosales, Mandy Stewart, Jorge Figueroa, Emarely Rosa-Dávila, Holly Hansen-Thomas, Luís Hernández, Christina Dearman, Eloise Kuehnert, Lal Rana, María Ortega, Karla Garcia Medina, Jenn Castillo, Kelly Partin, Dani Myers, Kio Kazaoka.

References

Bejarano, Carolina, Lucia López Júarez, Miriam Mijangos García, and Daniel M. Goldstein. 2019. *Decolonizing Ethnography: Undocumented Immigrants and New Directions in Social Science*. Durham, NC: Duke University Press.

Covey, Sean. 2014. *The Seven Habits of Highly Effective Teens*. New York: Simon and Schuster.

Del Monte, Katherine, and Max Benavidez. 2006. *Graciela's Dream/El Sueño de Graciela*. South Pasadena, CA: Lectura Books.

Dorner, Lisa M., Deborah Palmer, Claudia G. Cervantes-Soon, Dan Heiman, and Emily R. Crawford, eds. 2023. *Critical Consciousness in Dual Language Bilingual Education: Case Studies on Policy and Practice*. New York: Routledge.

Dyrness, Andrea, and Enrique Sepúlveda III. 2020. *Border Thinking: Latinx Youth Decolonizing Citizenship*. Minneapolis: University of Minnesota Press.

España, Carla, and Luz Yadira Herrera. 2020. *En Comunidad: Lessons for Centering the Voices and Experiences of Bilingual Latinx Students*. Portsmouth, NH: Heinemann.

Espinoza, Cecilia M., and Laura Ascenzi-Moreno. 2021. *Rooted in Strength: Using Translanguaging to Grow Multilingual Readers and Writers*. New York: Scholastic.

Fernandes, Leela. 2003. *Transforming Feminist Practice: Non-Violence, Social Justice and the Possibilities of a Spiritualized Feminism*. Berkeley, CA: Aunt Lute Books.

Fregoso Bailón, Raul Olmo, and Noah De Lissovoy. 2019. "Against Coloniality: Toward an Epistemically Insurgent Curriculum." *Policy Futures in Education* 17 (3): 355–369. https://doi:10.1177/147821031881920.

Freire, Paulo. 2000. *Pedagogy of the Oppressed*. New York: Continuum.

Hale, Charles. 2006. "Activist Research v. Cultural Critique: Indigenous Land Rights and the Contradictions of Politically Engaged Anthropology." *Cultural Anthropology* 21 (1): 96–120.

Heiman, Dan, Claudia G. Cervantes-Soon, Lisa M. Dorner, and Deborah Palmer. 2024. "Creating a Transformative Foundation for Dual Language Bilingual Education: Critical Consciousness at the Core." In *Handbook of Dual Language Bilingual*

Education, edited by Juan A. Freire, Cristina Alfaro, and Ester de Jong. New York: Routledge.

Heiman, Dan, Mariela Nuñez-Janes, Ivonne Solano, Cesar Rosales, and Maria Fernanda Ortega. Forthcoming. "Activism Against DLBE Gentrification at the School and Classroom Levels." In *Overcoming the Gentrification of Dual Language, Bilingual, and Immersion Education: Solution-Oriented Research and Stakeholder Resources*, edited by M. Garrett Delavan, Juan A. Freire, and Kate Menken. Tonawanda, NY: Multilingual Matters.

hooks, bell. 1994. *Teaching to Transgress: Education as the Practice of Freedom*. New York: Routledge.

Ladson-Billings, Gloria. 2021. "I'm Here for the Hard Re-Set: Post Pandemic Pedagogy to Preserve Our Culture." *Equity and Excellence in Education* 54 (1): 68–78.

Martínez, Pedro Santiago, Claudia Muñoz, Mariela Nuñez-Janes, Stephen Pavey, Fidel Castro Rodríguez, and Marco Saavedra. 2020. *Eclipse of Dreams: The Undocumented-Led Struggle for Freedom*. Chico, CA: AK Press.

Martínez-Napoles, Valeria. 2021. "Immigrant Journey to College." Accessed June 5, 2023. https://unt.zoom.us/rec/play/XymRi-PAIudapQo1RE0oY0MfaaRsRdFftBlNJj0UXwaKjDs-NP5uKg_JpqkYsmFwwVVHW88GNYlWuNlW.Y0z9VoObIJixT0_L?continueMode=true.

Nuñez-Janes, Mariela, and Dan Heiman. 2021. "Critical Pedagogy in Action." *Anthropology News* 62 (2): 22–25. https://www.anthropology-news.org/articles/critical-pedagogy-in-action/.

Nuñez-Janes, Mariela, and Mario Ovalle. 2016. "Organic Activists: Undocumented Youth Creating Spaces of Acompañamiento." *Diaspora, Indigenous, and Minority Education* 10 (4): 189–200.

Planella, Jordi. 2008. "Educación social, acompañamiento y vulnerabilidad: Hacia una antropología de la convivencia." *Revista Iberoamericana de educación* 45 (5): 1–14.

Sánchez, Maite T., and Ofelia García, eds. 2022. *Transformative Translanguaging Espacios: Latinx Students and Their Teachers Rompiendo Fronteras Sin Miedo*. Tonawanda, NY: Multilingual Matters.

San Pedro, Timothy. 2021. *Protecting the Promise: Indigenous Education between Mothers and Their Children*. New York: Teachers College Press.

Sepúlveda, Enrique III. 2011. "Toward a Pedagogy of Acompañamiento: Mexican Migrant Youth Writing from the Underside of Modernity." *Harvard Educational Review* 81 (3): 550–573.

Stringer, Ernest T., and Alfredo Ortiz Aragón. 2021. *Action Research*. Thousand Oaks, CA: Sage.

Villenas, Sofia. 2019. "Pedagogies of Being With: Witnessing, *Testimonio*, and Critical Love in Everyday Social Movement." *International Journal of Qualitative Studies in Education* 32 (2): 151–166.

PART II

Pragmatic Solidarity: Accompaniment in Binational, Bureaucratic, and Activist Spaces

CHAPTER 3

Mercados Dignos

Intergenerational Accompaniment among Indigenous Collectives in Guatemala

CARLOS ESCALANTE VILLAGRÁN, ANNA GREWE, AÍDA LÓPEZ, JUAN PACAY MENDOZA, SALVADOR PACAY MENDOZA, AND LAUREN HEIDBRINK

In response to the onset of the COVID-19 pandemic, Guatemalan president Alejandro Giammattei issued an executive decree curtailing mobility, gathering, and association. Restrictions included sporadic and sudden closures of local markets, a 4 p.m. curfew, suspension of public transportation, and road closures. The government returned to well-worn *mano dura* (iron fist) tactics, including exorbitant fines, jail time, and police harassment of those moving between communities. The national government subsequently closed down local, Indigenous markets where largely agrarian communities commercialize harvests and purchase food, claiming that the markets are "dirty," "unsanitary," and "disease-ridden." Giammattei encouraged people instead to shop at the country's three dominant supermarket chains, Walmart, PriceSmart, and UniSuper (La Torre/EconoSuper), claiming they are "cleaner" and "more organized." The use of disease-related tropes about Indigenous peoples and their practices is nothing new; these xenophobic discourses date to Spanish colonialism and the military dictatorship that inflicted genocide on Indigenous peoples during Guatemala's armed conflict from 1960 to 1996.

Although restricting movement seemed to be a well-founded decision in the context of the pandemic, this decision willfully ignored deeply racialized class inequalities that disproportionately impact rural, primarily Indigenous, communities. Take, for example, access to food. There is no access to large grocery stores in rural areas, and these stores are exponentially more expensive and are reliant on cash and credit cards to purchase goods. In contrast, local markets allow for greater flexibility to barter, exchange goods and services, and purchase on revolving credit based on longstanding relationships of trust between community members. The closure of local markets immediately compounded food insecurity plaguing the region. Further, many families risked defaulting on loans due to an inability to commercialize their products. That is, many vendors and farmers in the western highlands rely heavily on credit—from friends and family as well as banks, cooperatives, churches, and local moneylenders—to fund their harvests, sewing materials, and merchandise sold at local markets, often enlisting land as the only available collateral to secure loans. If unable to sell these goods at local markets and pay down loans, families confront the loss of ancestral lands (Heidbrink 2019, Johnson and Woodhouse 2018).

Within this dire context, *Colectivo Vida Digna*—a collective dedicated to affirming Mayan identities by supporting families from the countryside to fulfill their potential and to support the growth of their communities—initiated a two-pronged effort to address food insecurity and to reopen cantonal markets. In what follows, members of the collective reflect on the meanings and practices of accompaniment with U.S.-based anthropologist Lauren Heidbrink. Members of the collective include K'iche' spiritual guide Carlos Escalante Villagrán; Mam youth organizer Aída López; Tz'utujil agronomist Juan Pacay Mendoza; popular educator, social worker, and midwife Anna Grewe; and Tz'utujil financial auditor Salvador Pacay Mendoza. Lauren encountered the collective in 2010 through her longstanding work with the Guatemalan community in Chicago and later in her research with youth deported from the United States and Mexico to Guatemala. Now, Lauren collaborates on a variety of initiatives and serves as a board member. Through Zoom conversations, WhatsApp messages, and co-writing, we reflect on the multiple, overlapping forms of *accompaniment as praxis* centering Mayan Cosmovision. This includes walking with fellow community members during a global health crisis; the ongoing preservation and enactment of Indigenous lifeways in the face of extractivist exploitation, capitalist market economies, and the destructive impacts of deportation; and binational activism between an interdisciplinary collective and a U.S.-based scholar. Co-writing this chapter across multiple languages likewise illustrates accompaniment as it acknowledges and values the expertise and insights of collaborators by engaging as partners in the co-production of knowledge. This is particularly critical given how academic knowledge marginalizes Indigenous communities (Tuhiwai Smith 1999) and often ignores non-anglophone scholarship. Through collective conversation and co-writing, we contextualize emergent forms of solidarity embedded within struggles to resist longstanding state violence against Indigenous peoples.

* * *

En respuesta al inicio de la pandemia de COVID-19, el presidente de Guatemala, Alejandro Giammattei, emitió un decreto ejecutivo que restringía la movilidad, la reunión, y la asociación. Las restricciones incluyeron cierres esporádicos y repentinos de los mercados locales, un toque de queda a las 4:00 p.m., suspensión de todo el transporte público y cierres de carreteras. El gobierno volvió a las tácticas de mano dura muy conocidas, que incluyen multas exorbitantes, penas de cárcel, y acoso policial a quienes se movían entre comunidades. Posteriormente, el gobierno nacional cerró los mercados indígenas locales donde las comunidades mayoritariamente agrarias comercializan sus cosechas y compran sus alimentos, alegando que los mercados están "sucios," "no-higiénicos" y "plagados de enfermedades." A la vez Giammattei alentó a la gente a comprar en las tres cadenas de supermercados dominantes del país, Walmart, PriceSmart y UniSuper (La Torre/EconoSuper), diciendo que son "más limpias" y "más organizadas." El uso de tropos relacionados con enfermedades sobre los pueblos indígenas y sus prácticas no es nada nuevo; estos discursos xenófobos datan del colonialismo español y la dictadura militar que infligió el genocidio de los pueblos indígenas durante el conflicto armado en Guatemala desde 1960 a 1996.

Aunque restringir el movimiento parecía ser una decisión bien fundamentada considerando el contexto de la pandemia, esta decisión ignoraba deliberadamente las desigualdades de clase profundamente racializadas que impactan de manera desproporcionada en las comunidades rurales, principalmente comunidades indígenas. Tomemos, por ejemplo, el acceso a los alimentos. No hay acceso a grandes tiendas de comestibles en las áreas rurales que son principalmente indígenas, y estas tiendas son exponencialmente más caras y dependen del efectivo y las tarjetas de crédito por adelantado para comprar productos. Por el contrario, los mercados locales permiten una mayor flexibilidad para el trueque, el intercambio de bienes y servicios, y la compra con crédito renovable basado en relaciones duraderas de confianza entre los miembros de la comunidad. El cierre de los mercados locales agravó inmediatamente la inseguridad alimentaria que asola la región. Además, muchas familias corrían el riesgo de no pagar los préstamos debido a la incapacidad de comercializar sus productos. De hecho, muchos vendedores y agricultores del altiplano occidental dependen en gran medida del crédito–de amigos y familiares, así como de bancos, cooperativas, iglesias y prestamistas–para sobrevivir. Es decir, las familias solicitan crédito para financiar sus cosechas, materiales de costura y alimentos vendidos en los mercados locales, a menudo alistando la tierra como la única garantía disponible para obtener préstamos. Si no pueden vender estos bienes y pagar los préstamos, las familias enfrentan la pérdida de tierras ancestrales (Heidbrink 2019, Johnson and Woodhouse 2018).

En este contexto nefasto, el Colectivo Vida Digna—un colectivo dedicado a afirmar las identidades mayas apoyando a las familias del campo a desarrollar su potencial y apoyar el crecimiento de sus comunidades—inició un esfuerzo doble para abordar la inseguridad alimentaria y reabrir los mercados cantonales. A continuación, los miembros del colectivo reflexionan sobre los significados y las prácticas de acompañamiento con la antropóloga Lauren Heidbrink, quien ha colaborado con el colectivo durante más de una década. Los miembros incluyen al economista y guía espiritual maya-k'iche' Carlos Escalante Villagrán; la educadora maya-mam de jóvenes Aída López Huinil; el ingeniero agrónomo maya-tz'utujil Juan Pacay Mendoza; partera Anna Grewe; y el auditor maya-tz'utujil Salvador Pacay Mendoza. Lauren conoció al colectivo en 2010 a través de su trabajo con la comunidad guatemalteca en Chicago y más tarde en su investigación con jóvenes retornados de Estados Unidos y México a Guatemala. Ahora, Lauren colabora en una variedad de iniciativas y se desempeña como asesora. A través de conversaciones de Zoom, mensajes de WhatsApp, y la co-escritura reflexionamos sobre las múltiples y superpuestas formas de acompañamiento como praxis centradas en la cosmovisión maya. Esto incluye caminar con miembros de la comunidad durante una crisis de salud global; la preservación y promulgación en curso de las formas de vida indígenas frente a la explotación extractivista, los mercados capitalistas y los impactos destructivos de la deportación; y activismo binacional entre un colectivo interdisciplinario y un académico estadounidense. La co-escritura de este capítulo a través de varios idiomas también ilustra el acompañamiento, ya que reconoce y valora la experiencia y el conocimiento de lxs colaboradores como socios en la coproducción de conocimiento. Esto es particularmente crítico dado que el conocimiento académico marginaliza a las comunidades indígenas (Tuhiwai Smith 1999) e ignora la erudición no-anglófona. A través de conversaciones colectivas y co-escritura, contextualizamos formas emergentes de solidaridad incrustadas dentro de luchas contra una violencia estatal de larga data contra los pueblos indígenas.

* * *

Lauren: *What is the significance of the Guatemalan government shutting down local markets during the COVID-19 pandemic?*

Carlos: Cantonal markets and plaza days represent an important part of the economic legacy of Mayan communities. Since the time of our grandparents, markets have been spaces of commerce and of teaching and sharing of Indigenous knowledge and practice. These spaces were threatened not just by COVID-19 but also by a lack of resources and coordinated support from government authorities. We cannot allow our markets—our culture and identity—to disappear, but it's more. In our communities, we saw the unequal application of sanitary measures between markets and shopping centers as part of a coordinated effort of the state to eliminate local and cantonal markets, and by extension, Indigenous peoples in present-day Guatemala. The closures were an attempt to physically starve Indigenous communities—to limit access to food and care needed to survive especially during a time of crisis.

Lauren: *¿Cuál es la significancia de que el gobierno guatemalteco cierre los mercados locales durante la pandemia de COVID-19?*

Carlos: Los mercados cantonales y los días de plaza representan una parte importante del legado económico de las comunidades mayas. Son espacios de comercio desde la época de nuestros abuelos y de enseñanza e intercambio de saberes y prácticas indígenas. Estos espacios se vieron amenazados no solo por el COVID-19 sino también por la falta de recursos y apoyo coordinado de las autoridades gubernamentales. No debemos permitir que nuestros mercados, nuestra cultura e identidad, desaparezcan. Pero, es más. En nuestras comunidades vimos la aplicación desigual de medidas sanitarias entre mercados y centros comerciales como parte de un esfuerzo coordinado del estado para eliminar los mercados locales y cantonales, y por extensión, los pueblos indígenas en la actual Guatemala. Los cierres fueron un intento de matar físicamente de hambre a las comunidades indígenas: limitar el acceso a los alimentos que son necesarios para sobrevivir especialmente durante un momento de crisis.

Lauren: *In the early stages of the pandemic, what was happening in the communities where you live and work? How did Colectivo Vida Digna respond?*

Aída: Like so many people, we were in emergency mode. We quickly assembled *canastas dignas* (dignity baskets) which included a bag of groceries, cleaning products, and personal protective equipment. The government provided some *bolsas* (food baskets) mostly to its political base, but systematically excluded spiritual guides, midwives, and healers. The pandemic only exacerbated these longstanding experiences of marginalization and exclusion. So, we distributed *canastas dignas* to them as well as to families who live far from the city center of Quetzaltenango and who have limited access to basic goods due to restrictions on public transportation and the closures of local markets. The need was overwhelming. We launched a GoFundMe campaign with you and other friends in the U.S. to purchase additional materials from local farmers and vendors, and locally we gathered donated supplies from community members. Upon delivery, young people with whom we work—many of whom return and are returned from Mexico and the United States—gave culturally and linguistically-adapted public health *charlas* (talks) on hygiene and prevention of COVID-19. We delivered baskets to a total of 938 people in 18 communities and gave 139 talks. The support came at a critical time as the number of COVID-19 cases continued to rise in Guatemala.

Lauren: *En las primeras etapas de la pandemia, ¿qué estaba pasando en las comunidades donde vive y trabaja? ¿Cómo respondió el Colectivo Vida Digna?*

Aída: Como tanta gente, estábamos en modo emergencia. Rápidamente armamos canastas dignas que incluían una bolsa de víveres, productos de limpieza y equipo de protección personal. El gobierno proporcionó algunas bolsas principalmente a su base político, pero excluyó sistemáticamente a guías espirituales, parteras y curanderos. La pandemia solo hizo que esta realidad de marginalización y exclusión de larga data fuera más grave. Así, distribuimos canastas dignas a ellos y a las familias que viven lejos del centro de la ciudad de Quetzaltenango y que tienen acceso limitado a bienes básicos debido a las restricciones en el transporte público y el cierre de los mercados locales. La necesidad era abrumadora, por lo que lanzamos una campaña de GoFundMe con usted y otros amigos en los EE. UU. para comprar materiales adicionales de agricultores y vendedores locales y localmente recolectamos suministros donados por miembros de la comunidad. Al momento de la entrega, los jóvenes con los que trabajamos—muchos de los cuales regresan de y son retornados de México y Estados Unidos—brindaron charlas de salud pública adaptadas cultural y lingüísticamente sobre higiene y prevención del COVID-19. Entregamos canastas a un total de 938 personas en 18 comunidades y brindamos 139 charlas. El apoyo llegó en un momento crítico ya que el número de casos de COVID-19 seguía aumentando en Guatemala.

Lauren: *Why is the participation of youth so critical to Colectivo Vida Digna's accompaniment of communities?*

Aída: Canastas dignas and mercados dignos nurtured opportunities for young people to fulfill their responsibilities to community. Young people listened, shared, and raised awareness about COVID-19 and later about vaccines in a respectful way. They demonstrated their commitment to community through not only words but also their actions like delivering baskets of foodstuff and supplies to elders and healers, disinfecting public areas of the market, and organizing sanitation systems. Importantly, it created opportunities for intergenerational learning and exchange.

The pandemic put so many families in acute crisis but it also returned equilibrium to families. That is, with many parents out of work, unable

FIGURE 3.1 Aída López converses with a midwife in the community. Photo by Henning Sac.

to support their families financially or materially, everyone had to contribute to the family economy and survival, including young people. The hierarchy that we may see in some families with the father as head of household is a colonial idea; during the pandemic, young people worked alongside adults and women worked alongside men to care for each other. The actions of each family member reflect solidarity—not more or less than one another but as complementary equals within a family as they identified ways to support each other.

Lauren: *¿Por qué la participación de los jóvenes es tan crítica en los esfuerzos de Colectivo Vida Digna?*

Aída: Canastas dignas y mercados dignos fomentaron oportunidades para que los jóvenes cumplieran con sus responsabilidades con la comunidad. Ellxs escucharon, compartieron, y concientizaron a las comunidades sobre el coronavirus y luego sobre las vacunas en una manera respetuosa. Demostraron su compromiso con la comunidad no solo con palabras sino también con acciones como entregar canastas de alimentos y suministros a los ancianos y curanderos, desinfectar áreas públicas del mercado, y organizar sistemas de saneamiento.

La pandemia puso a tantas familias en una crisis aguda, pero también devolvió el equilibrio a las familias. Es decir, con muchos padres sin trabajo, sin oportunidad de sostener económica o materialmente a sus familias, todos tenían que contribuir a la economía y supervivencia familiar, incluidos los jóvenes. La jerarquía que podemos ver en algunas familias con el padre como cabeza de familia es una idea colonial; durante la pandemia, los jóvenes trabajaron junto a los adultos y las mujeres trabajaron junto a los hombres para cuidarse entre todos. La solidaridad se vio reflejada en las acciones de cada uno de los miembros de las familias, nadie era más ni menos, todos eran iguales, había una complementariedad entre las familias y en conjunto buscaron la manera de apoyarse.

Lauren: *Cantonal markets serve as many as 300 to 500 families. How did Colectivo Vida Digna scale-up to a project the size of mercados dignos (dignified markets)?*

Juan: Mercados dignos is the result of decades of walking with community—with guides, elders, young people, and their families. From *canastas dignas*, together we witnessed that the most affected in our community were Indigenous women, young and old, who work mostly in the informal sectors and in commercializing agricultural products. Single mothers, in particular, are highly vulnerable to state policies that overnight curtailed their earnings and restricted their ability to provide for their children. Women support the functioning of the markets, while also participating in planting, caring for crops, and harvesting and commercializing the products they take from the land. They garner great admiration and respect because they continue to practice ancestral knowledge of their grandmothers and grandfathers. Collaborating with them to create and protect more dignified spaces for vendors is fundamental to the work of Colectivo Vida Digna.

With the support of a grant that we wrote with you, we helped to create a system of daily cleaning and disinfecting; set protocols and posted signage for capacity, social distancing, and use of masks; and to establish hand sanitation stations. All the while, we facilitated communication between the market leadership and the municipal government. Working alongside a group of market women, we reaffirmed to the public and the government that the markets are clean and safe. As a result of these efforts, 142 vendors reopened their stalls, sold their products to

750 individuals, and provided food to an estimated 2400 beneficiaries in the month following its re-opening. Through this initiative, vendors, especially female vendors, made amends for the food insecurity in the region that resulted from the absence of a coordinated and inclusive government response.

Lauren: *Los mercados cantonales sirven de 300 a 500 familias. ¿Cómo escaló Colectivo Vida Digna a un proyecto del tamaño de mercados dignos?*

Juan: Mercados dignos es el resultado de décadas de caminar en comunidad—con guías, ancianos, jóvenes y sus familias. Desde canastas dignas, juntos fuimos testigos de que las más afectadas en nuestra comunidad eran las mujeres indígenas, jóvenes y adultas, que trabajan en su mayoría en los sectores informales y en la comercialización de productos agrícolas. Las madres solteras, en particular, son muy vulnerables a las políticas estatales que redujeron sus ingresos de la noche a la mañana y restringieron su capacidad para mantener a sus hijos. Las mujeres han logrado el sostenimiento de los mercados, además participan en las siembras, el cuidado de los cultivos, las cosechas hasta llegar a la comercialización de los productos que cultivan de la tierra. Es de mucha admiración y respeto porque no han dejado de practicar los conocimientos ancestrales que les han dejado las abuelas y los abuelos. Colaborar con ellas para lograr crear y proteger espacios más dignos para una vendedora o vendedor ha sido fundamental en el trabajo de Colectivo Vida Digna.

Con el apoyo de una pequeña subvención que escribimos contigo, establecimos un sistema interno y colaborativo de limpieza y desinfección diaria; establecimos protocolos y colocamos carteles de aforo, distanciamiento social y uso de máscaras; y se pusieron estaciones de saneamiento de manos. Mientras tanto, facilitamos la comunicación entre los líderes del mercado y el gobierno municipal. Trabajando junto a un grupo de mujeres del mercado, reafirmamos al público y al gobierno que los mercados son limpios y seguros. Como resultado de estos esfuerzos colaborativos, 142 vendedores reabrieron sus puestos, vendieron sus productos a 750 individuos, y proporcionaron alimentos a unos 2400 beneficiarios en el mes siguiente a su reapertura. A través de esta iniciativa, los vendedores–especialmente las mujeres–repararon la inseguridad alimentaria en la región que resultó de la ausencia de una respuesta gubernamental coordinada e inclusiva.

FIGURE 3.2 Vendor in the market. Photo by Colectivo Vida Digna (authors).

Lauren: *How does Vida Digna's ongoing accompaniment with returned youth and their families differ from accompaniment via mercados dignos?*

Anna: Much of our work includes accompanying young people and families affected by migration and deportation. Mayan Cosmovision teaches that life gives us experiences, and we have a responsibility to share these experiences with others. We sit with, listen to, and learn from families, and enter into dialogue. This may include members of our collective providing counseling and guidance, considering available options or opportunities, but we are always careful not to impose a single perspective. To be clear, it is not about asking a young person "What do you want to be when you grow up?" and training them in a specific job. Instead, we accompany them in finding their path so that they might contribute to their families and community. In the journey, we seek to break down barriers–to access school, services, or support; to reconcile misunderstandings across generations; or to advocate for a dignified life in the face of systemic discrimination. This type of accompaniment is an intimate and enduring relationship with families.

Mercados dignos and our collaboration with the market committee in Xela's historical market shares in the same ethic of accompaniment in practice, but the scale is different. The market leadership received us because they saw that we have been walking with communities for many years and that we were invested in dialogue rather than imposing ideas which unfortunately often is how nongovernmental organizations work in Guatemala. For twenty years, the market leadership has asked the municipal government to make basic infrastructure improvements, such as fixing the roof and improving drainage. The pandemic only exacerbated the barriers to persevering the markets. The market committee saw that we could exert additional pressure on the municipality to advocate for policy changes and for additional resources, barriers that are difficult to overcome in such a racist country.

Lauren: *¿Cómo se distingue el acompañamiento de Vida Digna a los jóvenes retornados y sus familias del dado por mercados dignos?*

Anna: Una gran parte de nuestro trabajo incluye acompañar a jóvenes y familias afectadas por la migración y la deportación. La cosmovisión maya enseña que la vida nos da experiencias y tenemos la responsabilidad de compartir estas experiencias con los demás. Nos sentamos, escuchamos, aprendemos de las familias, y entramos en diálogo. Esto puede incluir miembros de nuestro colectivo que brinden asesoramiento y orientación, considerando opciones y oportunidades, pero siempre tenemos cuidado de no imponer una sola perspectiva. Para que sea claro, no se trata de preguntarle a un joven "Qué quieres ser cuando seas mayor" y capacitarlo en un trabajo específico. En cambio, los acompañamos en la búsqueda de su camino para que puedan contribuir a sus familias y comunidad. En el camino, buscamos derribar barreras para acceder a la escuela, los servicios o el apoyo; reconciliar malentendidos entre generaciones; o abogar por una vida digna frente a la discriminación sistémica. Este tipo de acompañamiento es una relación íntima y duradera con las familias.

Mercados dignos y nuestra colaboración con el comité del mercado en el centro histórico de Xela comparten la misma ética de acompañamiento en la práctica, pero la escala es distinta. La dirigencia del mercado nos recibió porque vieron que llevamos muchos años caminando con las comunidades y que nos invertimos en dialogar y compartir ideas más que en imponer ideas que lamentablemente es como trabajan las organizaciones no gubernamentales en Guatemala con mucha frecuencia. Durante veinte años, el comité del mercado ha pedido al gobierno municipal que realice mejoras en la infraestructura básica, como reparar el techo y mejorar el drenaje. La pandemia sólo exacerbó las barreras para perseverar los mercados. El comité del mercado vio que podíamos ejercer una presión adicional sobre la municipalidad para abogar por cambios de política y recursos adicionales, barreras que son sumamente difíciles de superar en un país tan racista.

Lauren: *How are these two initiatives—canastas dignas and mercados dignos—situated within Colectivo Vida Digna's ongoing commitment to Indigenous economics and complementary economies?*

Salvador: At its core, Indigenous economies are rooted in essential values of cooperation, solidarity, and complementarity of talents and efforts. In this view, the "market" is not about competition, earnings and profit like capitalism professes, but about *mutual support* in which we center care for ourselves, our communities, the land and the universe. We recognize that we as individuals and as a collective learn more from others than they learn from us, and only by cooperating and collaborating can all people lead a dignified life. Because of wide-scale corruption and systemic discrimination, the Guatemalan state vis-à-vis the economy does not support Indigenous communities. We see time and again, the state actively seeking to marginalize and exterminate us—in its foreign policies, land policy, privatization of public services, extractivism, etc. The cantonal markets are a manifestation of our independence from the Guatemalan state and a space of freedom to express ourselves in our language, dress, and skills free of repression and judgment and to invest in both the value of the product itself as well as the knowledge and efforts that created it. In this way, we center the human experience not as a "consumer" in the "market" but as a contributor to community life. This is the ethic of care that animates our work with young people returning to Guatemala, with initiatives like *canastas dignas* and *mercados dignos*, and our ongoing efforts to create sustainable economies and communities for all original peoples.

Lauren: *¿Cómo se sitúan estas dos iniciativas—canastas dignas y mercados dignos—dentro del compromiso continuo del Colectivo Vida Digna con la economía indígena y las economías complementarias?*

Salvador: En esencia, las economías indígenas están arraigadas en valores esenciales de cooperación, solidaridad y complementariedad de talentos y esfuerzos. Desde este punto de vista, el "mercado" no se trata de competencia, beneficio, y ganancias como profesa el capitalismo, sino de apoyo mutuo en el que centramos en cuidado por nosotros mismos, nuestras comunidades, la tierra, y el universo. Reconocemos que nosotros como individuos y como colectivo aprendemos más de otras personas, y solo por cooperar y colaborar que todas las personas puedan llevar una vida digna. Debido a la corrupción a gran escala y la discriminación sistémica, el estado guatemalteco en relación con la economía no apoya a las comunidades indígenas. Vemos una vez tras otra, el estado buscando activamente marginar y exterminarnos—en su política exterior, política de territorio, privatización de servicios públicos, extractivismo, etc. Los mercados cantonales son una manifestación de nuestra independencia del estado guatemalteco y un espacio de libertad en donde expresarnos en nuestro idioma, traje y habilidades libres de represión y juicio e invertir tanto en el valor del producto en sí como en el conocimiento y los esfuerzos que lo crearon. De esta forma, centramos la experiencia humana no como un "consumidor" en el "mercado" sino como un contribuyente a la vida comunitaria. Esta es la ética del cuidado que alienta nuestro trabajo con los jóvenes que regresan a Guatemala, con iniciativas como canastas dignas y mercados dignos, y nuestros esfuerzos continuos para crear economías y comunidades sostenibles para todos los pueblos originarios.

Final Reflections / Reflexiones Finales

Our conversation elaborates how the praxis of accompaniment is multidimensional, intergenerational, and ongoing. We describe accompaniment as *multidimensional* across sites of struggle and solidarity, ranging from decolonizing gendered and generational dimensions of care in the home and marketplaces that Aída identifies, to the ways young people recognize and value Indigenous knowledge passed by elders and healers, as Juan describes, to working collaboratively with vendors to restore and preserve cantonal markets as sites of freedom and independence, as Salvador explains. In present-day Guatemala, accompaniment takes on temporal dimensions as it is situated within periods of racialized and gendered violence and displacement via Spanish colonialism (1524–1821), the plantation economy (nineteenth century), the armed conflict (1960–1996), and extractive neoliberal development (1980s to the present). The COVID-19 pandemic has only exacerbated the structural inequalities that attempt to push Indigenous peoples out of social and political life. As Carlos importantly historicizes, these intentional exclusions are reflected in the government's efforts to close markets in order literally and figuratively to starve Indigenous communities. The Guatemalan state's willful and ongoing failure to acknowledge, respect, and meet the needs of Indigenous communities shapes present conditions and simultaneously influences the aspirations and futures of individuals and communities seeking a dignified life. In response to these spatial and temporal dimensions, the collective describes accompaniment as necessitating a mindful, intentional, and inclusive presence rooted in an ethic of care.

For the collective, accompaniment likewise is *intergenerational.* In Mayan communities, young people value and are valued as critical contributors to the family and community life, as Anna and Aída illustrate. Through acts of consultation, collaboration, and exchange, young people demonstrated their respect and investment in Mayan Cosmovision, healing practices, and ways of knowing. So, too, healers and elders valued their knowledge and insights on new sanitary practices necessitated by the emergence of the COVID-19 pandemic and expressed gratitude for young people's recognition of the valuable roles they play in caring for communities. These acts of everyday care rehumanize and return young people—many of whom have been dehumanized by the United States and Mexican deportation regime—into the fabric of community life. Through a shared commitment to reciprocity, trust, and care, the collective affirms Indigenous identities of young people, their families, and their communities as part of their shared journey.

Importantly, accompaniment is an *ongoing process* during which Colectivo Vida Digna has walked with community for decades. This entails accompanying individual youths and their families following deportation, sharing ideas and entering into respectful dialogue; leveraging social and organizational power to advocate with municipal authorities in collaboration with the market's leadership; and responding to food insecurity through organizing. So, too, Lauren has leveraged her positionality as a U.S.-based, English-speaking scholar in order to raise visibility of Colectivo Vida Digna's important efforts via cross-border advocacy, fundraising and grant writing, hosting delegations to the United States, creating internships for university students, and accessing often-inaccessible spaces such as academic publishing. The degree and type of accompaniment fluctuates in response to moments of crisis or need and to new initiatives or undertakings in dialogue with members of the collective. Given that Indigenous communities around the world remain under sustained attack, continuity of accompaniment as praxis remains critical.

* * *

Nuestra conversación colaborativa elabora cómo el acompañamiento *en praxis* es un proceso multidimensional, intergeneracional y en curso. Describimos el acompañamiento como *multidimensional* a través de los sitios de lucha y solidaridad, que van desde la descolonización de las dimensiones generacionales y de género del cuidado en el hogar y los mercados que Aída identifica, hasta las formas en que los jóvenes reconocen y valoran el conocimiento indígena compartido y transmitido por los ancianos y los curanderos, como Juan describe, hasta las colaboraciones con los vendedores para restaurar y preservar los mercados cantonales como lugares de libertad e independencia, como explica Salvador. En Guatemala actual, el acompañamiento adquiere dimensiones temporales al situarse en períodos de violencia y desplazamiento racial y de género a través del colonialismo español (1524–1821), la economía de plantación (siglo XIX), el conflicto armado (1960–1996), y desarrollo neoliberal extractivo (década de 1980 al presente). La pandemia de COVID-19 ha exacerbado las desigualdades estructurales que intentan sacar a los pueblos indígenas de la vida social y política. Como importantemente historiza Carlos, estas exclusiones intencionales se reflejan en el intento del gobierno de cerrar los mercados municipales y cantonales y los días de mercado para literal- y figurativamente matar de hambre a las comunidades indígenas. La falta deliberada y continua del estado guatemalteco de reconocer, respetar y satisfacer las necesidades de las comunidades indígenas da forma a las condiciones presentes y, al mismo tiempo, influye en las aspiraciones y el futuro de las personas y comunidades que buscan una vida digna. En respuesta a estas dimensiones espaciales y temporales, el colectivo describe el acompañamiento requiere, según lo describe el colectivo, una presencia consciente, intencional e inclusiva, basada en una ética de cuidado.

Para el colectivo, el acompañamiento es igualmente *intergeneracional.* En las comunidades mayas, los jóvenes valoran y son valorados como contribuyentes críticos a la vida familiar y comunitaria, como ilustran Anna y Aída. A través de actos de consulta, colaboración e intercambio, los jóvenes demostraron su respeto e inversión en la cosmovisión maya, las prácticas de sanación y las formas de conocimiento. Así también, los curanderos y los ancianos valoraron sus conocimientos y percepciones sobre las nuevas prácticas sanitarias necesarias por el surgimiento de la pandemia de COVID-19 y expresaron su gratitud por el reconocimiento de los jóvenes del valioso papel que desempeñan en el cuidado de las comunidades. Estos actos de cuidado cotidiano re-humanizan y devuelven a los jóvenes, muchos de los cuales han sido deshumanizados por el régimen de deportación de Estados Unidos y México, al tejido de la vida comunitaria. A través de un compromiso compartido con la reciprocidad, la confianza y el cuidado, el colectivo afirma las identidades indígenas de los jóvenes, sus familias y sus comunidades como parte de su camino compartido.

Es importante destacar que el acompañamiento es un *proceso continuo* durante el cual Colectivo Vida Digna ha caminado con la comunidad durante décadas. Esto implica acompañar a los jóvenes individuales y sus familias después de la deportación compartiendo ideas y entablando un diálogo respetuoso; aprovechar el poder social y organizativo para abogar ante las autoridades municipales en colaboración con el liderazgo del mercado; y responder a la inseguridad alimentaria colectiva a través de la organización, el aumento de la visibilidad, la recaudación de fondos transfronteriza y la solicitud de subvenciones. Del mismo modo, Lauren ha aprovechado su posición como académica angloparlante basada en los Estados Unidos para aumentar la visibilidad de los importantes esfuerzos de Colectivo Vida Digna a través de la promoción transfronteriza, la recaudación de fondos y la redacción de subvenciones, la organización de delegaciones en los Estados Unidos, la creación de pasantías para estudiantes universitarios, y accediendo a espacios a menudo inaccesibles como la publicación académica. El grado y tipo de acompañamiento fluctúa en respuesta a momentos de crisis o necesidad y a nuevas iniciativas o emprendimientos en diálogo con los miembros del colectivo. Dado que las comunidades indígenas de todo el mundo permanecen bajo ataques sostenidos, esta continuidad del acompañamiento como *praxis* es fundamental.

References

Heidbrink, Lauren. 2019. "The Coercive Power of Debt: Migration and Deportation of Guatemalan Indigenous Youth." *The Journal of Latin American and Caribbean Anthropology* 24 (1): 263–281.

Johnson, Richard L., and Murphy Woodhouse. 2018. "Securing the Return: How Enhanced US Border Enforcement Fuels Cycles of Debt Migration." *Antipode* 50 (4): 976–996.

Tuhiwai Smith, Linda. 1999. *Decolonizing Methodologies: Research and Indigenous Peoples.* London: Zed Books.

CHAPTER 4

"Being-With," "Doing For," and "Doing With"

An Accompaniment Approach to Applied Research

SARAH B. HORTON

In January 2021, as I was engaged in interviews and advocacy work for a research project in Colorado, I received a call from my old friend, Elisabeta, an undocumented farmworker and participant in my previous project in California's Central Valley. Elisabeta had been my closest friend in the Valley, and I had long worried about how she had been faring during COVID—how she had handled the isolation, whether she and her five children had fallen ill, whether they protected her at work, how she paid her bills. When I answered the phone, I was dismayed to hear my friend—who had been strong, confident, and spirited—break into tears. While she had been driving to the fields some months before, her car had hit a chemical tank by the side of the road. In the crash, the chemicals burned her face and much of her body. Although Medi-Cal covered her hospitalizations and multiple surgeries, she had been cut off from humanity due to her disfiguration. "They did two surgeries on my face but my eyes, *my eyes*—my eyes are still not in the right place," she sobbed. Even more disabling was the residue of trauma—her grief and her deep sense of abandonment. "I need help," she had confided. And then, the most devastating statement from the woman who had left home at age fourteen to support her newly widowed mother, the woman whose courageous escapades I had followed and whose pluck I had long admired: "I'm not the person I used to be, Sara," she confided.

For years, I had been Elisabeta's companion, helper, and confidante; I had brought her children to the hospital to see her after her surgery for a brain tumor, I had helped her youngest son get free dental treatment from a mobile van, I was there when she and her husband split up. Over the years, we had established a deep bond of friendship that sprung from interpersonal affinity *and* from our uneven positionings: her capacity to teach me about farmworkers' realities, and my capacity to assist. But that spring, as I sought resources for Elisabeta from my COVID quarantine in Colorado, my ability to help was limited. I was combing the resources of Fresno County for Elisabeta even as I tried to balance the needs of the immigrant participants in my new project—connecting them with health care, rental assistance, legal assistance, and vaccines. And I was struggling with dark times of my own. My partner, who had three autoimmune conditions, had been unable to work for a month. My elderly father was showing signs of dementia and my mother, terrified of contracting COVID, had refused resources and care. As I sought to provide Elisabeta that sense of "being-with" that Yarris and Duncan compellingly describe in the introduction, I knew my efforts could do little to fill the chasm of her despair. And when I flew to California to visit my elderly parents in 2021, in my first cautious "post-pandemic" foray after fifteen months of quarantine, Elisabeta felt betrayed that I did not travel to the Valley to see her. "Why have you forgotten our friendship, Sara?" She asked. Her question cut like a knife.

Elisabeta's poignant question highlights the interpersonal and ethical dilemmas ethnographers face as we seek to enact accompaniment and strive to embody the principles of empathy, solidarity, and companionship that it entails. Elisabeta needed my friendship and help more than ever that spring, yet I was consumed by the multiple needs of my new companion-interviewees, my partner, and my aging parents. Her question raises the important issue of what forms solidarity can take in a research project—especially one entailing competing commitments to multiple participants—and how ethnographers move past the inevitable heartbreaks when accompaniment fails or is not enough. How do we maintain hope when accompaniment is but a salve to the harsh realities immigrants face? How do we balance empathic presence and solidarity with the urge to *do* and to help? How do we provide care without establishing expectations of presence and aid that are impossible to meet, and that risk undermining our participants' own resilience? And how might the kinds of engagement entailed by accompaniment change according to our own personal care obligations and over our life courses? These are issues that often arise in any long-term engagement with immigrants and yet are rarely addressed in any depth in traditional ethnographic work. By "center[ing] the relational dimensions of fieldwork" and attempting to "rehumanize the ethnographic encounter," as mentioned in the introduction of this volume, the framework of accompaniment provides an important opportunity to address them.

In this essay, I consider the different forms accompaniment took when integrated into a research project as well as the virtues and dilemmas of each. I have long believed that serving as a navigator—a kind of "researcher-cum-social worker" who helps participants navigate social service bureaucracies (Horton 2016, 185)—is an ethical imperative when conducting research with marginalized groups like immigrants. After all, if we do not pledge ourselves to assist our participants as we can, research with immigrants is merely an extractive enterprise that generates knowledge for academics' personal benefit (Bade and Martínez 2014; Bejarano et al. 2019). And yet Elisabeta's question highlights the thorny dilemmas that accompaniment-as-navigation raises: When does our role as brokers end? Is navigation sustainable over the long-term? And—in the most oppressive situations like Elisabeta's—how can navigation ever be "good enough" (see Bourgois and Schonberg 2009)? When, like Elisabeta, our participants face insurmountable conditions of structural violence, the urgency of *doing for* sometimes trumps all. Yet an accompaniment approach to research can also take other forms; aside from serving as navigators and brokers—*doing for*—we can work alongside our participants as co-conspirators and accomplices (see Gomberg-Muñoz 2018). Here I highlight the transformative potential of accompaniment-as-partnership in contrast with accompaniment-as-navigation. I suggest that when we are able to collaborate with our participants to create political change, accompaniment can transcend the verticality entailed in *doing for* and become a form of *doing with*.

Incorporating Accompaniment within a Research Project

Accompaniment means building bridges across divides of race, legal status, and class, forging relationships of solidarity and transferring privilege. As we listen to our companion-participants identify what is "at stake"

(Kleinman 1997) to them, accompaniment means aligning ourselves with them in struggling toward "what matters most" (Kleinman 1995). By holding another's emotional experience and making space for it, accompaniment can be a means of honoring the experiences of others, ensuring they feel seen and heard. And when we take on the concerns our participants identify and mobilize our resources toward ameliorating them, empathic listening and pragmatic solidarity can merge; accompaniment can transcend the personal through acts of advocacy and activism.

Within the context of a research project, then, the interpersonal and political goals of accompaniment can coincide. When our research addresses a concern central to our participants, and we work with participants on these issues individually as well, the goals of empathic listening, empirical research, and political change align. Here accompaniment shares much in common with engaged or public anthropology, as we use our empirical findings to document systematic barriers and press the state to change policy. We can also use our engagement in the policy process to inform our participants of new programs and assume the role of navigator as we assist participants in enrolling or applying for them. In this way, our research can inform our accompaniment of our participants and our care work can yield important empirical data; as Dvera Saxton puts it, accompaniment can be "a more politicized way of applying the classic ethnographic method of participant-observation" (Saxton 2021, 123). And, most compellingly, when our participants have the resources, capacity, and desire to engage in the political process, we can work alongside them in solidary action.

Below I consider the different forms solidarity took as I accompanied two participants in my recent longitudinal research project on immigrants' health care access in Colorado:[1] Amparo, whose son was deported, and Elisa, who lost her husband to COVID-19. I examine the virtues and ethical dilemmas raised by accompaniment as advocacy in moments of overwhelming crisis—moments like Elisabeta's. I suggest that

1. This chapter is based on fieldwork conducted as part of a collaborative grant funded by the National Science Foundation with Whitney Duncan, Co-PI, "Collaborative Research: An Ethnographic Study of Local-Level Policy Implementation Diversity" (#1827339). While I discuss my relationships with my research participants in this chapter, Whitney Duncan and I both engaged in these acts of micro-advocacy, care work, and political advocacy—sometimes together, and sometimes separately.

when we are able to be empathically present for our participants facing despair and intense structural violence—sharing the kind of "*digna rabia*" that Lopez, Kline, LeBrón, and Novak describe in chapter 8—we provide a sense of "being-with" that defies the tradition of distanced participant-observation. Working with participants to attempt to ameliorate such violence is the only ethical response. And yet, as Elisabeta's case shows, such advocacy raises important questions about the sustainability of our efforts, how we cope with failure, and how our relationships endure.

Accompaniment as Navigation

I have long believed that navigation is part of an unspoken ethical contract we establish when we work with populations in situations of steep social inequality. After all, members of marginalized populations often agree to share their lives with us with the implicit expectation that we serve as advocates—that we use our privilege as a shield (Horton 2016, 11). I believe ethnographers' obligations to our participants extend beyond merely publishing work sympathetic to our research participants' circumstances. When possible, our advocacy should have both political and personal dimensions, as we advocate not only on behalf of our participants at the political level but also assist them in the everyday ways our positionality allows.

Navigation can be emotionally rewarding, as we build deep, intersubjective bonds with our participants. As we assist our participants with the issues that matter most to them, we not only share a common cause but also become deeply emotionally invested in their priorities. As a white, cisgender, queer woman in my early fifties without children, I have the (relative) privilege of time and resources to expend on this kind of bureaucratic navigation. Yet as I age, I have found this kind of intensive advocacy on behalf of my research participants more challenging. The pandemic threw into relief the kinds of personal, ethical, and logistical challenges entailed by accompaniment-as-navigation. As the opening vignette shows, in moments of crisis—when our research participants, family members, and we ourselves face unprecedented challenges, crises which occur more frequently with time—accompaniment-as-navigation can quickly become unsustainable. Moreover, this kind of accompaniment raises a series of unresolved dilemmas: What happens to our relationships when our navigation is unsuccessful? Is the kind of deep emotional bond of commitment and engagement entailed by accompanying an individual sustainable long-term—both for our participants, and for us? For how long should we serve as accompagnateurs, and how do we avoid allowing the goal of *doing for* to eclipse the goal of *being and doing with?* The case of Amparo below helps us consider these questions.

Amparo

When I first met Amparo in the summer of 2018, she was warm and open, and I liked her immediately. Although my research project was focused on immigrants' health care access, Amparo made clear that a pressing concern for her was the well-being of the three children she had had to leave behind. Shortly after Amparo's husband abandoned her in Cuernavaca in 2004, Amparo found herself unable to support their children as a single mother. Shortly afterward, she migrated to the United States. Adán, her eldest—just five when her husband left—felt both departures keenly. After his father left, he often ran away, even hopping a bus with plans to visit him in Ciudad Juárez. "He would say, 'I don't want to live without my *papá*,'" Amparo remembered. After Amparo left, the object of his longing changed. In his teens, she said, Adán spoke of little else than obtaining a visa to be reunited with his mother.

Just four months after I met her, Amparo shared with me that her circumstances had dramatically changed. Her supervisor at the hotel she cleaned was able to persuade the hotel to hire Adán on an H2B visa, a temporary visa for nonagricultural workers. After thirteen years, she and Adán had finally been reunited. Adán's visa had been set to expire in October. But with their separation looming once again, Amparo had suggested he stay three months longer. "He's working days while I'm working nights; we've never had the time to talk," she had explained. And when I called her in April 2020—one month after COVID-19 had struck Colorado—I learned the worst had happened: Adán had been arrested. A neighbor called the police when her daughter, underage, sent him suggestive texts and he replied.[2] And because he no longer had a

2. Amparo and her lawyers suspect the teen sent these texts at the urging of her mother, who was attempting to use them to obtain a U visa—a visa available to those who cooperate with law enforcement to prosecute "criminals."

valid visa, ICE picked him up from the county jail. Having paid the bond for him to be released, Amparo had been standing at the entrance to the jail when they came, her jaw slack with shock as she witnessed her son being hauled away.

In the weeks and months that followed this devastating day, I—along with many others—became consumed with the acts of advocacy required to attempt to have Adán released from detention. Aligning myself with Amparo in the effort to secure her son's release seemed the only ethical response, but it was also a coping strategy; it helped me live with my own powerlessness. So, I did, and I *did*. When possible, I collaborated with Amparo, but—given our unequal positionings and my relative privilege—mostly I *did for*. The COVID-19 pandemic had only worsened the urgency of Adán's situation; detention centers had become a site of rapid viral spread. So I helped Amparo file a petition for humanitarian parole because of Adán's delicate health.[3] I wrote letters for her attorneys to argue for his release, documenting the impact of the loss of Adán's income on his citizen half-sisters. I tried—albeit unsuccessfully—to find Adán free legal representation, and documented his case for the statewide immigrant rights agency, which uses its database to track ICE activity and identify patterns of collusion with law enforcement.[4] And when Amparo's attorneys stopped returning her calls, there seemed no alternative but for me to assume the task of becoming her intermediary. Each week, I witnessed the fierce violence unleashed upon her by the legal system, attempting to document the insurmountable obstacles faced by families of deportees while sharing her *coraje* (rageful grief) as well as righteous anger, according to Lopez, Kline, Novak, and LeBrón in chapter 6 of this volume. Here, in theory, the goals of research and accompaniment aligned. However, in practice, melding the emotional engagement required by accompaniment and the distance required to record and document was a messy and at times sickening process. The

3. I am grateful to Whitney Duncan, co-editor of this volume and co-PI on this project, for connecting me with the American Friends Service Committee to file the petition for Adán's humanitarian parole, and for connecting Amparo to the support group for separated families, Ni1Más.

4. Amparo waited more than ninety minutes for her son to be released. This suggests that the Eagle County jail intentionally held him for ICE, despite the fact that ICE detainers have been ruled unconstitutional.

aporia in my fieldnotes speaks volumes—of days when I was too lost in despair to record the latest disappointment.

Accompanying Amparo both pragmatically and emotionally bonded us. And yet this kind of accompaniment can break your heart open—not only because of the emotional burden we share with our participants but also because of the frequent futility of our efforts at pragmatic solidarity. While my accompaniment provided Amparo some solace—some companionship in her inconsolable grief—I could do little to change the circumstances. Adán was ordered deported in May 2020. I accompanied Amparo one last time to the detention facility to drop off the money for Adán's flight and one change of clothes. We watched with anger and humiliation as detention facility agents inserted their fingers in each belt loop and each pocket—as though there might be drugs or a knife hidden there.

Like many other immigrants, Adán had been deported without having his day in court. According to staff at the immigrant rights agency, Adán was not alone in experiencing this injustice; many immigrants are apprehended because of criminal charges they are never given the opportunity to fight in court because they are deported before they can defend themselves. In Adán's case, the pandemic had deprived him of the possibility of acquittal. Because of the risk of contagion, the district attorney and county sheriff would not "writ" Adán so that he could appear in court. Meanwhile, because he "failed to appear" in court, the judge issued a warrant for his arrest. Out of all the injustices Amparo faced, this was by far the cruelest. "Because if he can't clear his name, how will he be able to get a visa to return?" she asked.

The months that followed were bleak for us both. Amparo clung to the possibility that if Adán could only have his case heard, the charge would be expunged, and he would be eligible to return with a visa. Each conversation I had with Amparo ended with the same request: that I write a letter to the criminal judge requesting that Adán have his day in court. Yet when I spoke to Amparo's lawyers, they warned that U.S. law is particularly harsh on adults—even if only eighteen years old—charged with "seducing a minor," and that having his day in court could sentence Adán to a lifetime in prison.

Although I view myself ethically bound to privilege my participants' priorities, I could not bring myself to write that letter. I sat with the discomfort and guilt for weeks. I sit with that moral queasiness, that disquiet, even still.

Amparo's case illustrates the kinds of deep intersubjective bonds that accompaniment-as-navigation can entail. Just as acts of advocacy emerge organically from an empathic relationship, they also deepen them. Serving as a kind of social worker immerses ethnographers deeply in attempting to mitigate the effects of structural violence on our participants, as we develop "skin in the game," so to speak. And yet Amparo's case also raises uncomfortable questions, highlighting the limits of partnership, the challenges of advocacy, and the tensions that emerge in our relationships when those whom we accompany have expectations that are impossible to fulfill. These are questions inherent in any long-term relationship of some intimacy—whether of ethnography, community-based research, accompaniment, or activism.

In retrospect, I think this case reveals some of the subtleties and challenges of the "social work" that I believe must be the cornerstone of fieldwork with immigrants facing harsh legal and structural violence. As Elisabeta's case suggests, maintaining close relationships—of both intimacy and of pragmatic assistance—with one particular participant may prove unsustainable over the long-term. To what extent does the accompaniment of immigrants across chasms of legal and class privilege establish expectations of aid that are impossible to fulfill? How do we maintain relationships when the promise of assistance upon which they are founded proves futile? How do we ensure that our accompaniment does not contract to a relationship of only service and immigrant dependency, undermining immigrants' own resourcefulness? And *can* we continue to intensively advocate on behalf of our participants as our obligations shift and our own care burdens mount? In opening the ethnographic relationship to scrutiny and urging humility and self-reflection, the paradigm of accompaniment asks us to consider these questions fully, even when our responses are unsettling.

An attempt to dissect how Amparo and I had reached this impasse illuminates some of the challenges of this kind of interpersonal accompaniment. In retrospect, I think that in this situation of extreme suffering, in which the urgency of mitigating further structural harm became a priority, my relationship with Amparo had contracted to one of protector and benefactor rather than companion and accomplice. In the crush of the overwhelming legal violence that tore Amparo from her son, the meaning of accompaniment was reduced to navigation alone, and the imperative of "doing for" eclipsed the radical solidarity of "doing with." Yet when the legal violence is less overwhelming and our participants have greater resources available to them, accompaniment can involve more horizontal rather than vertical forms of solidarity.

Accompaniment as Partnership in Action: The Ethnographer as Conduit

The radical solidarity inherent in the concept of "accompaniment" lies in its emphasis on unsettling the traditional power imbalances of the ethnographic encounter. As Bejarano et al. suggest (2019, 8), decolonizing the ethnographic encounter means "dismantl[ing] the subject/object dichotomy," underpinning it as we work with our participants as partners in action rather than as objects of knowledge. In so doing, we can defy the verticality inherent in ethnography—between "researcher" and "participant," "subject" and "object"—by working *alongside* our participants. This means positioning the immigrants with whom we work as experts and accomplices (Gomberg-Muñoz 2018) or, as Bejarano et al. put it, "learning *from* others rather than merely learning *about* them" (Bejarano 2019, 8). When the circumstances allow, then, accompaniment in the context of a research project can become more than mere companionship and navigation. Accompaniment can transcend empathic listening—"being-with"—and pragmatic brokering—"doing for"—to instead become a form of "doing with."

Elisa

My relationship with Elisa, an undocumented mother living in Carbondale, provides an example of how a research relationship can sometimes blossom into a horizontal partnership. I met Elisa in the summer of 2019 in her capacity as the health director for an organization that served the area's immigrant community. She was articulate and confident, proud of her work and eager to be of service. As I learned during that interview, her early years in the United States had been isolating and demoralizing. Trained as a physician in Mexico, Elisa was unable to practice because she lacked a U.S. medical license. She had emerged from her loneliness a decade ago through the very organization that later employed her; it offered free preschool for her toddler while also providing her with community. Less than six months after I met Elisa, however, Elisa lost her job. Concerned about the risks of employing the undocumented in a politically conservative area during the Trump administration—when raids were becoming more frequent—the organization's director fired her, along with all his undocumented employees. COVID-19 would strike four months after Elisa lost her job, only compounding her isolation at a time when she needed interaction the most.

When I called Elisa in the summer of 2020, I learned that her husband had fallen gravely ill in March—just as COVID-19 was beginning to spread throughout the county. Elisa tried to convince him to go to the emergency room, but he had refused. "And his oxygen began to fall, his blood pressure began to fall. And you know why he wouldn't go, Sara?" She said. "He wouldn't go so he wouldn't have to pay." With an intimate knowledge of the physiological processes occurring in his body, Elisa could do little else than witness his physical decline. "It was really difficult. . . . Trying to help him and seeing what was happening to his body but not being able to do anything. I just felt powerless," she described later. Elisa's husband was hospitalized for three days before he was transferred to a regional trauma center, where he spent three weeks and ultimately died.

Elisa spent the subsequent days in a haze, reeling from the sudden loss, trying to comfort her thirteen-year-old son, all the while facing a new depth of loneliness. It was during these days that she received her first bill: $63,000 for his three-day hospital stay. Although Emergency Medicaid would cover his treatment, state policy at the time required that undocumented immigrants obtain a physician's signature on a bureaucratic form certifying that the situation was indeed an emergency. If an onerous requirement in "normal" times, this became an impossibility during COVID-19—and ludicrous given her husband's death. "I wasn't allowed to enter because of COVID. You don't know what doctor treated him nor his number, and how are you going to get it?"

Elisa had worked, being paid under the table, as a medical assistant in a free clinic for undocumented immigrants, which ultimately allowed her to meet the state's requirements. Because of her job, she knew the enrollment coordinator at the local clinic, who was able to find the required county form. And she was fortunate enough to obtain the signature of the physician at the clinic where she worked, attesting that her husband's illness had indeed been an emergency. But Elisa was acutely aware that her connections made her unique. "How many others have been unable to meet these requirements?" she asked.

When I spoke with Elisa in June of that year, she was still lost in grief. We spoke about her feelings of powerlessness—of frantically taking her husband's vital signs yet feeling there was nowhere to go for help. Had her husband been confident that he could have received care in the emergency room without excessive bills, timely intervention could have potentially saved his life. She was outraged at the predicament in which she and her husband had found themselves and was committed to ensuring that other immigrants would not face this situation. When a *New York Times* reporter contacted me seeking immigrants willing to share their experiences of the pandemic and how they overcame them, Elisa immediately came to mind.

It turned out that this was the beginning of a mutually beneficial partnership. Elisa found the experience of seeing her story in print—her own narration of her husband's death and her feelings of disempowerment, stated *in her own words*—deeply empowering. Elisa helped me find participants for a survey my students conducted as part of a statewide campaign to expand Medicaid to the undocumented; in turn, I connected her with the working group of a state health advocacy agency aiming to reform Emergency Medicaid policy. "And you know what, Sara?" Elisa told me after the story ran, "I feel like my voice is being heard more, I'm participating more, I'm feeling more empowered."

Accompanying Elisa, then, not only involved holding space for her experience, validating her feelings of demoralization and rage, but also providing her a platform to pursue her concerns and elevate her story. In this example, then, accompaniment involved asserting solidarity by serving as bridge and as conduit, leveraging my privilege to promote Elisa's leadership by connecting her to advocacy organizations and reporters.[5]

5. Other examples of how researchers might promote immigrants' leadership and expertise include connecting them to advocacy organizations that can disseminate their stories and experiences. For example, I connected another participant with the

In short, when the circumstances allow, accompaniment can involve not only attempting to shield participants from structural violence but also leveraging our privilege to elevate immigrants' concerns and promote *their* leadership.

This relationship also changed me. Moved by Elisa's vulnerability in sharing the rawness of her experience with me—and by her story of bureaucratic violence amid profound personal loss—I made reforming state Emergency Medicaid policy a central goal of my research. Working together with an advocacy association for local community clinics, I wrote a brief for the state with examples of immigrants who had not been offered Emergency Medicaid, including Elisa. We pushed for multiple reforms to the state's Emergency Medicaid policy: not only for removing the physician letter requirement, but also for extending the eligibility period for Emergency Medicaid to twelve months so that immigrants on cancer treatment and dialysis would not have to requalify each month, leading to discontinuous care. I had learned from my research that many undocumented immigrants in new immigrant destinations had never been offered Emergency Medicaid despite being potentially eligible, and then had to apply retroactively, often finding themselves disqualified by the ninety-day eligibility window imposed by the federal government. So, together with Dr. Lily Cervantes—a physician whose research had persuaded the state to allow Emergency Medicaid to cover dialysis—I urged the state to allow immigrants to qualify for Emergency Medicaid in advance, just as they might for any other insurance. Lily had the state connections, and the insight into the policy process, that allowed us to time and direct our advocacy successfully. Meanwhile, my research provided the empirical evidence of the need for policy change. Elisa served as a sounding board as she was able. Working together with a shifting coalition of partners, we were ultimately successful on all three counts.

In this way, then, accompaniment can transcend empathic listening and navigation to entail mutual partnership, and this in turn can make interpersonal solidarity a source of political change. Nevertheless, it is important to recognize that not all of our research participants have the resources and capacity to mobilize in this way. In many ways, Elisa was

National Immigration Law Center so that she could share the impact on her citizen children of her exclusion from the CARES Act stimulus in a press conference.

unique. Already well-connected in the community due to her work for the immigrant advocacy agency, and adept at understanding health care policy due to her training as a physician, Elisa was well-positioned to be a co-conspirator and accomplice.

Elisa's story illustrates the way that affect—in this case, the shared righteous indignation at Elisa's predicament—can be productively blended with the empirical findings of applied research to create change. In this case, the large sample size provided by my research project abetted our cause, as the multiple examples I provided of immigrants facing barriers to obtaining Emergency Medicaid proved persuasive. Thus, unlike accompaniment-as-navigation—which is often only feasible with small sample sizes and focuses on changing circumstances for individual participants—this is an example of far-reaching policy change that was accomplished under the auspices of a large-scale applied research project. Yet while traditional fieldwork aims to "eliminate" personal bias, an accompaniment approach to research recognizes that affective commitments can enrich, rather than contaminate, the scientific method (see Lopez, Kline, Novak, and LeBrón in chapter 6 of this volume). Moreover, the two can be blended toward strategic ends. Indeed, the example in this case of successful advocacy combined the shared rage generated by accompaniment with the "authoritative" findings produced by applied research, as we strategically mobilized as a coalition to submit the research reports I drafted to the state.

Final Thoughts

If accompaniment is worth doing, this is because of the extremity of structural violence that makes it incumbent. Our acts of advocacy may fail, and our best efforts at partnership and companionship may founder. And when those with whom we work face overwhelming hardships, the urgency of immediate assistance sometimes trumps all. The case of Amparo illustrates the dilemmas raised by the intensive emotional accompaniment and navigation that I believe should be the cornerstone of any research with immigrants. It raises thorny questions about the sustainability of the emotional commitments we establish as ethnographers as well as about the long-term sustainability of the promise of aid our presence implies—questions that have no easy answer.

And yet, at the same time, accompaniment-as-navigation can serve as the emotional wellspring for our ethical commitments as ethnographers, as we share the righteous indignation of our participants. When our participants have the time, resources, and desire to engage in the political process, we can work alongside them in solidary partnerships. Indeed, as Elisa's story shows, the goals of empirical research, political change, and interpersonal solidarity can sometimes coincide, as the shared rage generated by accompanying immigrants serves as the springboard for applied investigations. In these moments of mutual partnership and policy strategizing, the imperative of *doing for* can yield to the radical solidarity of *doing with*.

References

Bade, Bonnie, and Konane Martínez. 2014. "Full Circle: The Method of Collaborative Anthropology for Regional and Transnational Research." In *Migration and Health: A Research Methods Handbook*, edited by Schenker Marc, Castañeda Xóchitl, and Rodríguez-Lainz Alfonso, 306–326. Oakland: University of California Press.

Bejarano, Carolina, Lucia Lopez Juárez, Mirian A. Mijangos García, and Daniel M. Goldstein. 2019. *Decolonizing Anthropology: Undocumented Immigrants and New Directions in Social Sciences*. Durham, NC: Duke University Press.

Bourgois, Philippe, and Jeffrey Schonberg. 2009. *Righteous Dopefiend*. Oakland: University of California Press.

Gomberg-Muñoz, Ruth. 2018. "The Complicit Anthropologist." *Journal for the Anthropology of North America* 21 (1): 36–37.

Horton, Sarah. 2016. *"They Leave Their Kidneys in the Fields": Illness, Injury, and "Illegality" Among US Farmworkers*. Berkeley: University of California Press.

Kleinman, Arthur. 1995. *Writing at the Margin: Discourse between Anthropology and Medicine*. Berkeley: University of California Press.

Kleinman, Arthur. 1997. "'Everything That Really Matters': Social Suffering, Subjectivity, and the Remaking of Human Experience in a Disordering World." *Harvard Theological Review* 90 (3): 315–336.

Saxton, Dvera. 2021. *The Devil's Fruit: Farmworkers, Health, and Environmental Justice*. Newark, NJ: Rutgers University Press.

CHAPTER 5

Accompaniment in Activist Spaces

Solidarity at Ethnography's Edges with an Immigrant Bond Fund

KRISTIN E. YARRIS

In the pre-pandemic summer of 2019, I spent many hours sipping iced tea in coffee shops in downtown Eugene, strategizing with other local activists in a newly formed, all-volunteer group (the Oregon Asylum Network, or OAN) to aid asylum seekers about how best to allocate our limited resources. Since late 2018, volunteers with the group had been working to resettle asylum-seeking friends they had met during solidarity encounters at the U.S.-Mexico border—this resettlement work requiring resources at every step, from legal fees to housing assistance. One major obstacle had become raising the funds needed to post bond in order to secure the release of asylum seekers who had been detained in immigration detention centers, leading the group to form a subcommittee to address this issue through the creation of a revolving bond fund, supported by donations, which could pay bond fees for asylum seekers looking to resettle in Eugene. While several thousand dollars had been raised for the bond fund, another challenge was deciding which OAN-sponsored asylum seekers would receive support through the bond fund. With limited resources available and so many asylum seekers forcibly detained and needing assistance, how could the bond fund be set up in a fair and equitable way that aligned with the group's broader mission to achieve justice for asylum seekers and other immigrants? In this chapter, I take the invitation to consider accompaniment as a grounding practice and perspective through which to consider my ethnographic involvement with immigration bond fund work. Here, my positionality vis-à-vis accompaniment is like a tool of engaging in activist spaces, aligning myself with local solidarity groups fostering welcome and inclusion for precariously statused migrants. In what follows, I offer a background for understanding immigrant detention and bond funds that is rooted in antiracist and abolitionist perspectives. I then explore the dynamics of deservingness that played out in the bond fund work I was involved with in Oregon, considering these dynamics from a perspective of engaged, activist involvement, in which I was entangled in the very activism that brought these tensions to the foreground. My aim is to foreground how accompaniment can be a mode of ethnographic engagement in activist spaces that opens avenues for understanding dynamics of immigrant inclusion, rights, and justice.

My ethnographic positioning in and through activist involvements with immigrant rights efforts is an explicit one—that is, I acknowledge I am accompanying organizational, social, and political processes that shape possibilities for inclusion and belonging for asylum seekers and other migrants. This is to say that my reflections about accompaniment here are drawn from work not necessarily alongside migrants themselves but, rather, from working with local activists who seek to offer welcoming and inclusive spaces for asylum seekers and other immigrants. (A similar approach is taken by Sarah Horton in chapter 4.) My hope is that this reflection on accompaniment in activist spaces sits productively alongside other types of accompaniment presented in this volume, opening opportunities for thinking about the ways in which accompaniment can take place in organizational, institutional, and policy spaces, in addition to at individual and community levels.

Here I focus on one specific effort of the OAN: establishing a bond fund designed to release asylum seekers and other migrants from detention. Essentially, the way immigration bond funds operate is through initial capitalization (in this case, through donations), paying bond to release detained migrants from detention, and then, once immigration legal cases are resolved, reinvesting the returned bond monies into the fund on a revolving basis. However, as I describe below, the CBF has not yet reached a level of capitalization and functionality to be able to operate in this way and help all those who need assistance. In fact, as they have struggled to raise sufficient funds, bond fund volunteers have engaged in difficult deliberations over who to help, and these very deliberations reveal the ways in which local humanitarian efforts may unwittingly reproduce the inequities of care and deservingness embedded in state systems of migration governance.

Hierarchies of Care and Histories of Racist Exclusion

While my ethnographic observations in this chapter are grounded in the experience of accompanying one local immigrant bond fund in Oregon, the contestations over deservingness and care for asylum seekers described herein must begin with a broader (albeit necessarily brief) review of the history of immigrant detention in the United States. This history helps reveal how hierarchies of deservingness are built into carceral treatment of migrants by the U.S. government and, in a broader way, how racist histories of governance are foundational to the structures of citizenship in the United States.

From critical refugee studies, I find important grounding for a critique of the ways in which immigrant rights and solidarity work among volunteer humanitarians (Humphris and Yarris 2022) may reproduce (even unintentionally) the hierarchies of deservingness embedded within immigration policy, laws, and state forms of migration governance (Malkki 2005, Ticktin 2006, Watters 2019). For instance, this may take the shape of imposing racialized or cultural assumptions about which migrants are more worthy of membership in the destination state and reinforcing these assumptions through volunteer efforts such as refugee resettlement. This dynamic over deservingness is at play in the bond fund work I describe in this chapter—as activists faced realities of limited resources, they struggled to imagine more inclusive possibilities about who the bond fund could assist. These dynamics also intersect with the boundaries of nationality, race/ethnicity, class, and gender, and the ways the U.S. immigration legal system reinforces these social categories as grounds for meriting inclusion. For this reason, engaged anthropological analysis of the interactional dynamics among volunteer activists involved with the bond fund contribute to a critical, discursive, much-needed decolonizing perspective (Harrison 2010) on the ways U.S. immigration policies past and present reproduce racist and xenophobic constructions of belonging.

My assessment of an immigration bond fund in this chapter also draws from abolitionist, antiracist framing. In the U.S. political context, immigration detention is one of many carceral tactics employed against asylum seekers and other precariously statused migrants. Thinking about the work of CBF through an abolitionist frame pushes me to situate contemporary immigrant rights organizing within a broader critique of the history of carceral systems in the United States and the ways they have functioned as gatekeepers of citizenship by doling out punishment, alleging criminality, and offering belonging along lines of race, color, national origin, and class. My accompaniment work with movements for immigrant justice and community health equity in Oregon has pushed me to make connections between racist laws that historically excluded African Americans from the state with contemporary policies and practices that exclude immigrants as well as counter-hegemonic efforts to expand immigrant inclusion and belonging.

According to Mark Harris, a scholar of African American history, racialized exclusion was written into the founding of Oregon state law. Nineteenth-century laws made slavery illegal but also criminalized Black bodies by requiring them to leave the state. An 1844 law mandated that "any Black who fails to leave [Oregon] can be arrested, and, if found guilty, be sold to the lowest bidder for service to someone who agrees to remove them from the state within six months after that service expires. That person must post bond of at least a thousand dollars" (Harris 2007). This historical assessment demonstrates how the state's racialized codification of certain bodies as criminal or illegal led to an early implementation of bond payments. In other words, the founding of the state in Oregon was premised upon drawing lines of racialized exclusion and capturing bodies of color in carceral systems in order to leverage bond payments for their release. The parallels between this racist history of Black exclusion in Oregon and the contemporary immigration detention system are unmistakable. Further, Harris describes how "At the time these exclusion laws were passed, there were about 200 free Black people in Oregon . . . and [they essentially became] illegal" (Harris 2007). In other words, since the nineteenth century, state laws circumscribe illegality, constricting legal opportunities for citizenship along racialized lines and rendering those deemed unlawful as removable or deportable.

Contemplating Harris's critique of racial exclusion as it was codified in Oregon law from the time of the state's founding compels a consideration of contemporary migrant exclusion within a broader history of racial exclusion. This reflection is obviously grounds for a much longer discussion than the present chapter permits. Nonetheless, an antiracist critique of citizenship and belonging helps provide context for the ways in which struggles for African American freedom and justice across U.S. history lay the groundwork for understanding contemporary contestations over citizenship, power, and racial exclusion into the present (Mezzadra 2020). For an anthropology of accompaniment, contestations over racial privilege, navigating power dynamics within social movements, and engaging with antiracist social justice critiques are central to the challenges of engaged ethnography with contemporary immigrant rights movements. At the same time, accompaniment in these contested spaces of intersectional activism is generative of insights into antiracist discourses and organizing practices for migrant inclusion.

In thinking about this sort of intersectional, abolitionist approach, I am inspired by the 2022 book *Abolition. Feminism. Now.*, in which Angela Davis and colleagues argue for a reinsertion of feminist praxis within abolition movements. Pointing out the ways in which feminists have at times unwittingly reinforced carceral responses to gender-based violence, for example, the authors argue for connecting abolitionist principles into feminist work in order to avoid punitive responses that reinforce racist inequities in policing and imprisonment (Davis et al. 2022). Drawing connections to the present discussion, this critique raises questions about how efforts to help release certain immigrants from detention might unwittingly reinscribe other migrants within narratives of racialized criminality. Furthermore, as I outline below, immigration bond fund organizing can productively be linked to intersectional and antiracist efforts to abolish the prison industrial complex and to radically reimagine community safety, care, and belonging.

Detention and Migration Governance in the United States

Immigrant detention is a form of political cruelty, which Christina Beltrán (2020) has argued is apparent in the ways white privilege in the

United States relies on the unjust and *cruel* treatment of immigrants (and thereby sustains "white democracy"). In an important recent history of U.S. immigration detention, Elliot Young connects the incarceration of noncitizens across the twentieth century to contemporary deportation regimes (Young 2021). An outlier when considering the treatment of asylum seekers in global perspective, in the United States, many asylum seekers are subject to prolonged periods of detention as part of their journeys (FitzGerald 2019). While a full exploration of detention as a tool of immigration governance is beyond the scope of this chapter, I outline several key features of detention in order to provide a background for understanding the Cascades Bond Fund.

Since the nineteenth century, the detention and forced removal of migrants in the United States has reflected racialized notions of which migrants are deemed worthy of residing in the territory and which can be forcibly dispelled. For instance, in 1893, the U.S. Congress gave immigration officers the discretionary power to determine which migrants to detain and which to release, beginning a system of bond payments to securitize migrants' release from detention that echoes the bond system described earlier that was a part of Oregon's racial exclusion laws. Bond payments were further justified and codified into the 1952 Immigration and Nationalization Act. By the 1980s, the privatization of immigrant detention in the United States was expanding exponentially, with large federal contracts given to private companies like GEO Group and Corrections Corporation of America (now CoreCivic) (FFI, n.d.). The immigration detention system steadily expanded into the twenty-first century, with federal spending on detention exceeding three billion dollars in 2019 (MPI 2020).

The United States holds the nefarious distinction for having the world's largest immigrant detention system, with over two hundred facilities incarcerating more than half a million people (García Hernández 2019). Whether operated by private companies or by municipal governments (as jails), immigrant detention centers house different categories of displaced people, among them asylum seekers, undocumented migrants detained in the interior, and all categories of immigrants deemed by ICE to having committed an infraction. Currently, an average length of stay in U.S. immigration detention facilities is approximately one month; however, migrants may be released after a day, or they may be held for over a year—with cases varying by facility, region, and the disposition of immigration judges.

While obtaining accurate and current information about immigrants held in detention centers is difficult, the Syracuse University-hosted TRAC (Transactional Records Access Clearinghouse) System uses FOIA (Freedom of Information Act) requests to make data on immigration courts and detention centers publicly available. From TRAC, we learn, for instance, that bond fees set by immigration judges vary widely by Executive Office for Immigration Review (EOIR) court, region, and city, ranging from $1,000 to over $25,000 (with an average of about $5,000). To date in 2021, there were more than 950,000 immigrants in detention seeking bond, with only half of them granted bond-based release. By nationality, the largest groups of immigrants granted release from detention by bond are Mexican, Guatemalan, Salvadoran, and Honduran. Furthermore, according to TRAC, the number of cases and the average wait time to settle a case in U.S. immigration courts has steadily increased since 2005, reaching a backlog of over 1.4 million cases by 2021. Average wait times in 2021 were one thousand days, or approximately three years (TRAC n.d.).

Engaging with the immigration detention system means contending with its illogics and cruelty at every turn. For instance, while some asylum seekers are admitted at the border without detention, others may be released from detention quickly with low bond amounts, while still others are detained for months or even years with bond amounts set extraordinarily high. The capriciousness of asylum decisions reflects a number of factors, including individual border officer and immigration judge (IJ) prejudices as well as country geopolitical affiliations with the United States (partly explaining why Cubans or Nicaraguans are treated differently/detained with less regularity than Haitians or Hondurans). It may also be that the presence of local humanitarian groups aiding asylum seekers—whether legal advocates, human rights observers, or volunteer sponsors—influences IJs' decisions related to bond and release.

The Oregon Bond Fund

The volunteer humanitarians involved with establishing the Oregon bond fund struggle to make sense of the capricious and cruel realities of the ever-expanding carceral system that ensnares asylum seekers. The Cascades Bond Fund (CBF) was formed as a subcommittee of the broader OAN for asylum seekers, which formed in 2018 largely in response to the "caravans" of Central American migrants arriving at the U.S.-Mexico border, and about which I have written elsewhere (Humphris and Yarris 2022). As volunteers sought to sponsor asylum seekers in one Oregon metropolitan area, they increasingly realized that raising funds needed to post bond for migrants' release from detention was an essential part of their broader resettlement efforts. I was involved in initial meetings of the CBF subcommittee across the fall and winter of 2019, when it was becoming increasingly apparent to volunteers in the network that the legal fees associated with resettling asylum seekers in our community exceeded volunteers' capacity to pay. Conversations started about organizing a revolving bond fund, with donations raised to pay bond and release asylum seekers from detention, and later on—once asylum cases were resolved legally—those bond fees "revolving" back to the fund. At the outset, the CBF was a collaborative effort across three local social service organizations: the first, a nonprofit organization with longstanding ties to Latinx and immigrant families and communities; the second, a faith-based organization that had a legal services program for immigrants and refugees; and the third, the new volunteer-based network group. All three groups saw the bond fund as a promising resource to aid the communities of migrants they served. The initial aim of the CBF, therefore, was broad and referred to "assisting all immigrants in detention with ties to [the county where the fund originated]."

I was involved in CBF meetings across 2019 and until early 2020, when the COVID-19 pandemic paused our work. I considered this work "ethnographic," insofar as I was participating in social movement meetings, observing dynamics between volunteers, taking fieldnotes on my observations, and connecting my on-the-ground reflections to broader anthropological understandings of migration, immigration governance, and solidarity and care. But as I showed up to meetings and danced with the dynamics of doing-too-much or not-doing-enough as a volunteer myself, I was also aware that this type of ethnography in activist spaces may cultivate novel anthropological sensibilities. As an activist, I can be committed to the process of developing systems that support immigrant rights and inclusion, while as an ethnographer, I can reflect on the complicated dynamics of deservingness and care at play in this work.

In my work with this immigrant bond fund, I somewhat uncomfortably navigated my role as an academic—an anthropologist of migration who might offer historical and comparative context for understanding the processes of asylum seeking—while also being grounded in my positionality as a community member with experience volunteering with local migrant rights and social service organizations, including two of the three organizations founding the CBF. In my field notes from CBF meetings, I would jot down observations such as, "Deliberations in the meeting over whether to formalize this work as a 501c3—I'm remaining agnostic," which captured my desire to help, but not to overly determine the course of the work. Nonetheless, feeling strongly that our local bond fund should be connected to broader national efforts, I did propose to the committee early on that CBF connect to Freedom for Immigrants (FFI), an established nonprofit organization based in the San Francisco Bay Area that coordinates immigration bond funds across the United States (FFI n.d.). I then became centrally involved in a series of meetings with FFI where we established their role as the fiscal sponsor for CBF, which meant FFI would accept donations and coordinate the administrative and legal processes for asylum-seeker release from detention. Looking back, this was a moment in my accompaniment of the bond fund process where I think I assumed more of an organizer role than an accompanier role; however, the lines between these positionalities are thin and easy to confuse.

Personally, and particularly during the summer of 2019 when I was not teaching at the university, I allowed the bond fund work to become all-encompassing. Between attending CBF meetings, coordinating conversations between the three stakeholder groups, reaching out to national organizers including FFI, helping draft documents of incorporation, and working on the eventual application process, bond fund activism became my full-time summer (unpaid) work. I would note here that I never considered this work to be explicitly research; instead, I thought of it primarily as activism—meaning I never completed an IRB (institutional review board) process nor did I complete a consent process for any individual to participate in the study as a human research subject or interviewee.

However, I also knew that, as an engaged anthropologist interested in immigrant rights movements, my involvement with CBF was offering me rich ethnographic insights on the dynamics of local volunteer humanitarianism and solidarity work. While I was concerned that I may be doing too much as a volunteer with CBF, my real reason for beginning to withdraw from the work had to do with the summer drawing to a close and facing a fall term heavy with university teaching and service responsibilities. I note this here because I am aware of the ways in which our academic positions both afford us flexibility to engage in activist and other accompaniment work, but also entail very real constraints on our ability to sustain volunteer engagements, especially when these are not easily connected to or legible as "research." In my case, my impending fall term responsibilities also coincided with a number of troubling dynamics emerging in the CBF committee, all of which pushed me to articulate to other volunteers that I needed to transition to a less significant role in the work as of fall 2019.

Bond Funds and Intersectional Organizing

One of the motivations behind connecting our Oregon bond fund to FFI was to engage explicitly with the broader political project of ending immigrant detention. In 2020, even as the COVID-19 pandemic put a pause on in-person CBF meetings, our local activist communities were contending with the summer of activism inspired by the Black Lives Matter movement and calls for addressing systemic racism across U.S. institutions. In response, some bond fund committee members began to seek ways to connect our work within immigrant advocacy communities to broader abolitionist work for racial justice. One inspiring example of this type of intersectional work is found in Believers Bail Out, a project of anthropologist-activist Maryam Kashani and colleagues who created a bond fund upon Islamic principles of solidarity and debt forgiveness, and who organized across racial communities, building bridges to other anti-carceral efforts in Chicago (Believers Bail Out n.d.). These sorts of intersectional organizing efforts have not yet been realized by CBF.

In Oregon, CBF is the only existing immigration bond fund. There was a pretrial bond fund in the Portland area, Portland Freedom Fund, which worked to bring attention to the racial and class inequities built into the cash bail system for criminal defendants (OPB 2022). I had hoped to help connect CBF to the work of this fund in order to start conversations about intersectional organizing; however, this idea was hampered by the pandemic and by my return to full-time faculty responsibilities, as mentioned above. As a result, the CBF has yet to realize its potential to connect to antiracist, abolitionist bond fund organizing, and there is great potential in connecting immigration bond funds to broader movements for racial justice and carceral reform. At minimum, applying an abolitionist frame to the work of the immigration bond fund encourages a careful consideration of how advocacy on behalf of immigrants in detention may, even unwittingly, reinforce carceral approaches to immigration policy—for instance, when federal laws such as VAWA (Violence Against Women Act) or other legislative forms of "relief" are predicated on the criminality of brown and Black (immigrant) male bodies, or when securing legal status for some migrants (those deemed more deserving) relies on reinforcing the illegality and criminality of others (deemed less so).

Immigration Bond Funds: Potentials and Pitfalls

In addition to the challenges we faced in intersectional organizing, the bond fund encountered much more pragmatic pitfalls. While we had raised about six thousand dollars by the end of 2019, this amount was far short of what was needed to release the many asylum seekers the network hoped to resettle in our community. Additionally, as staff of migrant-serving organizations and legal-service providers across Oregon got word of our bond fund, we received multiple requests to post bond for other migrants in need of assistance that we had to deny because our fund was designed to only aid immigrants with ties to our local community. The bond fund simply lacked the resources needed to help everyone who needed assistance. This reality forced difficult conversations in the bond fund committee over who to help and reckoning with the impossible question of how to fairly determine who is worthy of release from detention when so many migrants are trapped in the carceral regime of the U.S. immigration system.

By accompanying the bond fund organizing work, I was able to observe many unsettling conversations that took place among volunteers and centered on this tension of deciding who to help. For instance, in early meetings of the bond fund committee, there was broad support that the fund should aid the release of all immigrants with ties to our county—whether they are new asylum seekers from Central America sponsored by network volunteers, undocumented Mexican-origin residents with long ties to the community and detained by ICE, and/or Indigenous Mam-speaking refugees served by the faith-based legal services program. In other words, the initial aim of the bond fund was to be as inclusive as possible, encouraging potential donors to consider all groups as equally worthy of freedom from detention.

Despite these activist and inclusionary aims, fissures soon emerged. For example, in our contested considerations of how to determine eligibility for the bond fund, contradictions that mirrored broader forms of state exclusion surfaced. Some thought that network-affiliated donors should be able to earmark donations to particular asylum seekers that network members were sponsoring. On the other hand, nonprofit staff working with the longstanding immigrant-serving organization countered that donations should be pooled and that a fair and open application process—with a review committee representative of the different organizations involved in the fund—should review applications and determine priority based on transparent criteria. This led to trying conversations in bond fund meetings where volunteers confronted the mismatch between the magnitude of need and the reality of our limited funds. In my field notes from these meetings where we sought to determine eligibility for the fund, I often wrote a common refrain repeated by exasperated volunteers: "We just can't help everyone." Accompanying these processes of bond fund organization meant that I too was wrapped up in the often emotional deliberations over how to move forward in the face of the magnitude of need and the limited funds of CBF. If I had merely interviewed volunteers, I'm not certain I would have understood how heart-wrenching these deliberations truly were.

So . . . who would be helped? With limited available resources, the bond fund committee made the decision to help just those asylum seekers sponsored by network volunteers. One argument in support of this decision was that, since network volunteers were doing most of the fundraising, "their asylum seekers"—those that they were sponsoring—should be prioritized. Other deliberations about whether to help women with children before single men, or relatives of asylum seekers already resettled before migrants with no family ties to the community, ensued. As of this writing, just two individuals—both sponsored by network volunteers—have received bond fund assistance. Perhaps unwittingly, then, the bond fund is reenacting state systems of migration governance and enforced exclusion, reinscribing hierarchies of care, through its deliberations and determinations over which migrants are morally worthy of inclusion and care.

Accompaniment in Activist Spaces

Some of the tensions that emerged across the formation of the bond fund hold lessons for the potential pitfalls of community-engaged anthropology and accompaniment within activist spaces. Inevitably, important organizing questions emerge through which we may feel pushed to take sides based on our own values or principles. Within the bond fund, some of the tensions that emerged reflected underlying issues of race, class, gender, and power, and, as Lopez and colleagues similarly describe in chapter 6 of this volume, it was impossible for me to remain neutral in the face of these troubling dynamics and unsettling positionalities.

For example, one staff member of the Latinx social service organization who was herself young and Latina found herself doing much of the administrative work of the group: taking notes, setting up shared cloud drives, and organizing meetings. When she and I brought attention to this dynamic within the bond fund committee, our request for a more equitable division of the service labor needed to operate the fund was met with defensiveness and pushback by some of the older, white, male volunteers. Feeling gaslit, this young woman understandably decided to stop participating in the bond fund. This essentially led the initial organizational structure to fall apart, since the only members left were network volunteers.

These tensions are certainly not uncommon in immigrant rights activist work, and they require us as anthropologists engaged in these spaces and accompanying this work to deliberate carefully over our involvement and the choices we make in these movements. I felt very uncomfortable with some of the decisions being made by the bond fund organizing committee to selectively prioritize asylum seekers sponsored by network volunteers over longstanding undocumented immigrants with ties to our community served by the social service organization. My displeasure with the departure of the Latina staff person aggravated my discomfort, and coincided with my return to fulltime academic responsibilities, all of which led me to step away from active involvement in the bond fund by early 2020.

Concluding Comments

This chapter engages with immigrant detention as one form of structural violence shaping unequal access to opportunities for asylum seekers and other precariously statused migrants and with bond fund activism as one mode of solidarity contesting the boundaries of exclusion that circumscribe social and political opportunities for migrants. In writing this chapter, I am aware how my accompaniment of the bond fund both emerges out of my ability to assume the role of volunteer-activist due to my personal identities as a white female with a history of involvement in movements for immigrant justice, but also how the professional identity I carry with me in this work, as an academic anthropologist and university professor, produces its own tensions in the field. At times the power and prestige of my title and positionality generate opportunities for engagement, while other times, they represent barriers to an aligned experience of accompaniment. Overall, I understand accompaniment as blurring boundaries between fieldwork and activism, research and praxis, theory and lived experience. Furthermore, I write this chapter aware that my colleagues in bond fund work are among the potential audience for this conversation, and therefore my critique is intended at all times to be deeply respectful of volunteers' commitment to solidarity with asylum seekers and other migrants and always intended to contribute to immigrant justice work in constructive ways.

People's lives hang in the balance of institutional and legal systems that foreclose opportunities for belonging and violently exclude through detention, deportation, and prolonged waiting. While local, volunteer efforts to assist asylum seekers can help individuals navigate cruel state-imposed processes en route to resettlement and belonging, these humanitarian efforts can also reinforce cruelty by unwittingly reproducing racist hierarchies of exclusion. Moreover, in the face of the enormity of contemporary forced migration flows—with over one hundred million people as forced migrants worldwide (UNHCR n.d.)—the U.S. asylum process only offers relief to a small fraction of the humans being pushed from their homes by economic insecurity, political instability, and climate change in the twenty-first century.

Rather than reinforcing exclusionary and racialized narratives of state regimes of migration management, how can volunteer humanitarian efforts and local activists broaden the boundaries of membership and inclusion? One possibility comes out of immigration bond fund activism, such as when advocacy groups like Freedom for Immigrants frame the work of releasing individual migrants from detention as explicitly connected to a broader political and antiracist aim of ending immigrant detention and carceral systems of care more broadly. Furthermore, an abolitionist perspective can deepen the intersectional analysis of immigrant bond funds, helping these efforts engage across racial, ethnic, and national origin lines to broaden the political potential of immigration bond funds and to imagine political alternatives to carceral forms of care for immigrants.

Grounded in an anthropology of accompaniment and speaking from an authentic space of reflection on my engagement with the bond fund, I am full of regret that I have been unable to pursue this line of activist work more fully. Of course, the COVID-19 pandemic brought the bond fund work and the broader work of the Oregon Asylum Network largely to a halt in early 2020, and network meetings (since being held remotely) only resumed regularly in late 2021. Still, I have not reengaged with bond fund work as fully as I might have wished, and my remorse about this is among the many consequences of how accompaniment draws us emotionally into relationships and commitments in the communities we work with. One final reflection I would offer based on my experience with the bond fund is that writing itself may be a form of accompaniment, as Hansen and Robles Robles represent in their chapter in this volume. In my case, writing this chapter pushed me to reconnect to CBF and other bond-fund activists. In a broader way, by writing about our anthropological experiences with immigrant activism, we share the lessons of activism and solidarity with broader audiences and can together thereby imagine alternative, more inclusionary futures.

References

Believers Bail Out. n.d. Believers Bail Out. Accessed August 10, 2022. https://believersbailout.org/.

Beltrán, Cristina. 2020. *Cruelty as Citizenship: How Migrant Suffering Sustains White Democracy*. London: University of Minnesota Press.

Davis, Angela Y., Gina Dent, Erica R. Meiners, and Beth E. Richie. 2022. *Abolition. Feminism. Now*. Chicago: Haymarket Books.

FitzGerald, David Scott. 2019. *Refuge beyond Reach: How Rich Democracies Repel Asylum Seekers*. New York: Oxford University Press.

Freedom For Immigrants (FFI). n.d. Freedom for Immigrants. Accessed August 21, 2022. https://www.freedomforimmigrants.org/.

García Hernández, César Cuauhtémoc. 2019. *Migrating to Prison: America's Obsession with Locking up Immigrants*. New York: The New Press.

Harris, Mark. 2007. Oral History Interview. Interview conducted by Karen Olsen as part of a "Teaching American History" grant. August 1, 2007. Archived at Lane County History Museum, Eugene, OR. Collection L2016.040, Disc 1.

Harrison, Faye V. 2010. *Decolonizing Anthropology: Moving Further toward an Anthropology for Liberation*, 3rd ed. Arlington, VA: American Anthropological Association.

Humphris, Rachel, and Kristin E. Yarris. 2022. "Welcoming Acts: Temporality and Affect among Volunteer Humanitarians in the UK and USA." *Migration and Society* 5:75–89.

Malkki, Liisa. 2005. *The Need to Help: The Domestic Arts of International Humanitarianism*. Durham, NC: Duke University Press.

Mezzadra, Sandro. 2020. "Abolitionist Vistas of the Human. Border Struggles, Migration, and Freedom of Movement." *Citizenship Studies* 24 (4): 424–440.

Migration Policy Institute (MPI). 2020. "As #DefundThePolice Movement Gains Steam, Immigration Enforcement Spending and Practices Attract Scrutiny." Migration Policy Institute. https://www.migrationpolicy.org/article/defundthepolice-movement-gains-steam-immigration-enforcement-spending-and-practices-attract.

Oregon Public Broadcasting (OPB). 2022. "Portland Freedom Fund Continues Mission to Help BIPOC Defendants Post Bail." Oregon Public Broadcasting. September 7, 2022. https://www.opb.org/article/2022/09/07/portland-freedom-fund-continues-mission-to-help-bipoc-defendants-post-bail/.

Ticktin, Miriam. 2006. "Where Ethics and Politics Meet: The Violence of Humanitarianism in France." *American Ethnologist* 33 (1): 33–49.

Transactional Records Access Clearinghouse (TRAC). n.d. "Immigrant Court Bond Hearings and Related Case Decisions." TRAC Immigration. Accessed August 15, 2022. https://trac.syr.edu/phptools/immigration/bond/.

United Nations High Commissioner for Refugees (UNHCR). n.d. "Figures at a Glance." The UN Refugee Agency. Accessed September 10, 2022. https://www.unhcr.org/en-us/figures-at-a-glance.html.

Watters, Charles. 2019. "Forced Migrants: Inclusion, Incorporation, and a Moral Economy of Deservingness." In *Routledge International Handbook of Migration Studies*, 2nd ed., edited by Steven Gold and Stephanie Nawyn, 81–89. Oxford: Routledge Press.

Young, Elliott. 2021. *Forever Prisoners: How the United States Made the World's Largest Immigration Detention System*. New York: Oxford University Press.

PART III

Methodologies of Accompaniment: Affect, Stories, and Solidarity

CHAPTER 6

A Public Health of Accompaniment

WILLIAM D. LOPEZ, NOLAN KLINE, NICOLE L. NOVAK, AND ALANA M. W. LEBRÓN

As researchers and advocates who study the health impacts of immigration enforcement, we have engaged deeply with families and communities impacted by surveillance, arrest, incarceration, and deportation. Sometimes we engage as researchers gathering formal data during periods of time that our universities' institutional review boards have formally approved. Other times, we engage as volunteers with immigrant-serving organizations, doing whatever is needed, from making spreadsheets to giving rides and providing community lectures on immigration policy. And other times, we have no goal beyond simply being with friends and neighbors whose lives we care deeply about, and who may sometimes just happen to have been part of our studies. We have thus formally documented and personally borne witness to the legal violence (Abrego and Menjívar 2011) and lasting damage of state-funded and propagated surveillance, separation, and removal.

As public health researchers with training in anthropology, we have relied on our training to conduct rigorous research to better understand the multiple factors that shape the life trajectories and health outcomes of those in immigrant communities. The research skills we gained from training in each of these fields have provided us with the tools we need to conduct, for example, studies on differences in birth weight among white and Latino infants following a historic worksite raid (Novak, Geronimus, and Martinez-Cardoso 2017), self-rated health, trauma, and fear of deportation after a home raid (Lopez et al. 2017; 2018), the community-wide fallout of immigration worksite raids (Collins et al. 2022; Lopez et al. 2022), deportation and its spillover effects on communities (Lopez 2019; Lopez and Castañeda 2022), photo identification as a social determinant of health (LeBrón et al. 2018; 2019), and how police practices and immigration laws come together to create unique forms of harm (Kline 2018).

This work is exhausting physically, mentally, and emotionally. We love the communities and people with whom we work, and we bristle at unjust systems that harm them. We bring our full selves—sometimes accompanied by our families—to the research, and we sit with the grief and rage that naturally extend from documenting the suffering of those we love. We have worked both directly with impacted communities as well as with the agencies and organizations dedicated to serving them. Sometimes this makes our work seem slow and plodding compared to that of our peers, and our CVs and résumés comparatively empty, as the work of driving someone to an immigration appointment or taking over the urgent-response scheduling system while someone is sick doesn't have any clear promotional value in the academy. But we are, finally, at peace with our work, and the toll it takes on our personal and professional lives.

Yet this hasn't always been the case. Like many other academics, we spent years wrestling with the components of our work historically viewed as antithetical to the "objective" social science research expected of public health professionals. In this chapter, we describe the evolution of the framework that guides our research and advocacy in public health, what we call a public health of accompaniment. A public health of accompaniment suggests that, rather than researching from above, we walk alongside, prioritizing the health and well-being of communities and walking together toward the mutually shared goal of health equity. We begin with an overview of the tenets of public health that have allowed us to center community collaboration in our work. We draw from anthropology's postmodern, postcolonial turn to describe how we integrate emotions—especially grief and rage—into our public health work. We build on Zapatismo to foreground how we have come to move from research, through grief, and into growth, collaboration, creativity, and progress. We then present four essays that interrogate our "moments of discomfort" (Petillo 2020), reflecting on how exploring—rather than rejecting—these moments of discomfort served as "opportunities for feminist scholarship" (Petillo 2020, 20) that allowed us to develop a public health of accompaniment. We end by describing a public health of accompaniment and providing recommendations to public health practitioners heavily invested in the well-being of the communities at the center of their research.

Centering Communities: Researcher Engagement in Public Health

As public health–trained researchers, we have found multiple frameworks to be essential in grounding our work and connecting it to action. To make our work legible to the broader field of public health, we have often used community-based participatory research (CBPR) as a shorthand for the commitments we hold and collaborations we value. Under a traditional public health model, CBPR conceptualizes researchers and community members as equal partners in all phases of the research process; it includes elements of co-learning and shared decision-making to achieve long-term goals (Israel et al. 2017). At the heart of CBPR is the focus on responding to local community problems and needs and investing in long-term relationships.

The foundational principles of CBPR are not dissimilar to the principles that undergird the perspectives of engaged and activist anthropology (Hale 2006; Speed 2006), and indeed CBPR's foundations include feminist research practices, postcolonial theory, and Freirean praxis (Wallerstein and Duran 2017). Notably, however, the field of public health has insufficiently advanced an explicitly activist research perspective. Further, unlike anthropology, the field has not had the equivalent of a "postmodern turn" or "postcolonial moment" that included an inward, reflexive assessment of the field overall.

Community-engaged research (CEnR) in public health has largely been used as an umbrella term to capture collaborative relationships between academics and community members (Luger, Hamilton, and True 2020). Like CBPR, CEnR can focus on increasing community capacity for collaborative research, which may result in formalized and institutionalized collaborative agreements and efforts to design research interventions or evaluate programs (Luger, Hamilton, and True 2020).

These methods, however, have felt insufficient to us. To us, CBPR and CEnR still primarily feel like research is the goal of a relationship rather than prioritizing the relationship itself. Further, these methods do not explicitly emphasize a shared political goal of liberation, challenging injustice, and ending root causes of oppression—values that orient our work, motivate our action, and inform why we pursue graduate degrees. More than doing CBPR or CEnR, our work is rooted in rage against injustice and grief for human suffering, as we describe next. Similarly, more than being bound by a moment in time that can end when research activities cease and "products" are disseminated, our work includes a persistent connection with the people we care about.

Grief and Rage: The Necessity of Emotion in Public Health

"Suffering" is not a word often seen in public-health discourse. Instead, members of the field typically use "morbidity" and "mortality," "years of life lost," "disability adjusted life years," "self-rated health," "self-efficacy," or "medical adherence." These measures are important and allow for public-health professionals to investigate specific relationships between social context, policy, and health outcomes. But they can also result in the "medicalization of distress" (Thangadurai and Jacob 2014), reducing the most vulnerable moments of human lives—like suffering, death, and illness and the patterns in which they exist—into variables to be intellectualized.

But with proximity to the communities at the center of our research, it becomes increasingly impossible to distance ourselves from the suffering we document. And documenting this suffering inevitably results in intense emotions, like grief, exasperation, despair, uselessness, frustration, and, especially, rage. Research has occasionally acknowledged the toll of the emotions extending from research, describing it, for example, as vicariously experienced trauma (Smith et al. 2021) or "compassion stress" (Rager 2005) that drains us psychologically while taking a toll on our bodies (Dunn 1991).

While early social science attempted to cast emotion as antithetical to "objective" research, most social science disciplines have problematized the notion of objectivity and drawn on a range of frameworks to integrate emotion into research. With important differences, these frameworks include positionality, reflexivity, "socially responsible science" (Krieger 1999), and others. These frameworks provided us with guidance in considering the ways in which we could work through emotions without impacting the methodological rigor of our work. However, methodological rigor was not our primary concern. We weren't worried that our emotions would dilute the science. We were instead worried that ignoring our emotions would be inauthentic and mask the urgency of the research behind scientifically justified emotional vapidity.

As public health workers with training in the humanities, we thus turned to the work of anthropologists to guide the intense emotions we were experiencing. Anthropology took a drastic turn toward embracing emotion in fieldwork following the notable essay by Renato Rosaldo (2004), "Grief and a Headhunter's Rage," in which he documents the death of his wife during fieldwork and the essential role of his own grief in understanding the rage of the Ilongot "headhunters" he and his wife were observing. Rosaldo described this rage as "an emotional force" so intense as to make its motivation for headhunting self-evident, contrasted with the anthropological proclivity for "thick description, multivocality, polysemy, richness, and texture" (Rosaldo 2004, 167). That is, emotion may be the answer itself, not simply a tool to guide one's methodology and analysis.

Rosaldo's essay challenged many of the positivist structures embedded in anthropology at the time. Ruth Behar, a Cuban American feminist anthropologist, further argued for the integration of one's subjective, emotional experience into their writing. In her essay, "What Renato Rosaldo Gave Us" (Behar 2012), Behar posits that Rosaldo allowed academics to finally embrace their emotional side, creating an "academy where our hearts didn't have to be checked at the gate as if they were a danger to institutions of higher learning" (Behar 2012, 205). To Behar and others that followed, emotion is what makes ethnographies worth reading and worth writing. In her book *The Vulnerable Observer* (1996), she summarizes concisely that "anthropology that doesn't break your heart just isn't worth doing anymore."

Later, Gilberto Rosas (2021) explores the "emotional force of rage and sadness" in "Grief and Border-Crossing Rage," a moving piece set in his hometown of El Paso, Texas. Rosas was engaged in fieldwork on family separation in El Paso in August 2019 when a white nationalist opened fire in a local Walmart, killing twenty-two people. The shooter later stated in a manifesto that his goal was "to kill as many Mexicans as possible." In his own rage and grief, Rosas writes that he, a cisgender man of color, must approach rage, grief, and similar emotional forces carefully, lest he be read as a "hot-headed macho, a man ostensibly consumed by irresponsible, dangerous, corporeal urges and other passions such as lust and envy" (Rosas 2021, 118). He thus draws on other authors to help redirect his grief and anger at the witnessing of the slaughter of his own community, authors including Audre Lorde, Cherríe Moraga, and Gloria Anzaldúa. Rosas lastly draws from Zapatismo, a tradition that bridged the emotional challenges of our work to our desire to use our research to work toward the goals of health equity.

We had each learned about the Zapatismo tradition at various points in our lives and work. The Zapatistas created a public health system rooted in shared labor in response to centuries-long disenfranchisement and theft of Indigenous land. They described their response to this theft as "*digna rabia*," loosely translated as "dignified rage," and argued that this rage was the natural, expected, logical response to wide-scale structural violence. However, they did not see this rage as antithetical to growth but instead as an essential component to mobilization, organization, and "the building of new social relationships, the creation of another way of doing things and another way of loving" (Alonso 2009). Embracing *digna rabia* in our work allowed us to accept rage and grief at the injustices we documented—feelings that were necessary and natural, and not antithetical to our desire for future mobilization.

Moments of Discomfort, Moments of Growth

In the following four short essays, we each reflect on a "moment of discomfort" (Petillo 2020) in which we felt the work we were doing was contrary to our training as public health researchers and scientists. In preparation for this chapter, we shared and read these four essays among each other, discussed these moments, and drew out the critical threads we believed together formed our model of a public health of accompaniment.

William Lopez: A Postdoc with a Driver's License

On a regular Wednesday in February 2017, I drove Guadalupe to the United States Citizenship and Immigration Services (USCIS) Field Office to take her biometrics for a U Visa application. It was about a forty-five-minute drive from where she lived in a new mobile home, still very small, but bigger than the apartment she moved into after her original living space was raided by ICE and the police in November 2013.

Since first meeting Guadalupe, I had spent hours with her and her family, learning from her and her children what it was like to be left behind after law enforcement used a no-knock warrant to kick in her door and take all the men—including her brother and nephew—out of their lives. Guadalupe and I had eaten together, formally recorded multiple interviews, and informally talked many times besides. Our oldest kids, by then about eight years old, even enjoyed the occasional Pokémon card trading session together.

By the time Guadalupe and I drove down Interstate 94 to Detroit, I was done with the IRB-approved data collection that resulted in my dissertation. But my relationship with Guadalupe wasn't on the same academic time frame, nor was the U visa application and approval for which we were desperately hoping. So, even though no formal research product would likely result from this interaction, I of course drove her anyway when she asked.

I knew in some way that I was not doing what efficient researchers were "supposed" to do: make every interaction result in something, a paper, a presentation, a grant, something. But Guadalupe didn't need a presentation. She needed something much simpler that I was able to provide: she needed a ride to Detroit. And while I was a researcher, a post-doc, a writer, an advocate, while I was one day going to be a subject-matter expert on the very experience that Guadalupe had lived through, none of that mattered. What mattered was beautifully simple: I had a driver's license. I spoke English. I wasn't taking time off an hourly job to drive her around. If I got pulled over, I had a loose idea of what to do, couldn't be detained myself, and knew enough about the U visa process to emphasize that it already involved collaboration with the police and therefore nothing could come of an arrest.

I realize now that what I was engaging in was some early version of a public health of accompaniment, a public health that nimbly moves to address trauma in many forms, from the structural to the interpersonal, from the evidence-based to the narrative of suffering unfolding in front of you. I realize that, while it was because of my research that I met Guadalupe, I was now walking with her, accompanying her through the systems of injustice with which she struggled every day. Why would I spend years of my life mapping out a system of oppression if not to share with others the safest path along the map? I also realized that our goals were beginning to crystalize and align. In this case, our goal was the shared advancement of our community—our Washtenaw County Latino community—and, in this particular instance, the advancement of our community meant that Guadalupe would get a visa, be in the United States, and raise her kids after so much had been taken away. While she probably would not use these words, I would suggest that our mutual goal in that moment was walking together toward health equity.

Nolan Kline: The Movement Family

At the 2017 Equality Florida Gala in Orlando, leaders of the organization gathered to a stage at the Orlando Museum of Art to announce the Voice of Equality award, a recognition of work done to empower LGBTQ+ individuals. That year's winner was QLatinx, a social, sexual, gender, racial, and immigration justice organization that focuses on empowering LGBTQ+ individuals who experience intersecting forms of oppression. QLatinx emerged after the 2016 Pulse club shooting, when a gunman entered the club on Latin night and fatally shot forty-nine patrons and injured dozens of others. In the aftermath of what had been the deadliest shooting in U.S. history that also disproportionately affected people identifying as LGBTQ+ and Latinx, QLatinx started a journey of collective healing and empowerment following grief and trauma.

QLatinx quickly became a leader in Central Florida for advancing intersectional social justice efforts across the region. My involvement with QLatinx began in the fall of 2016—a few months after the Pulse shooting. Organization members became, and continue to be, close friends. As a researcher trained in medical anthropology and public health who has a methodological attachment to engaged and activist anthropology, my commitments to QLatinx blended personal and professional interests.

The night QLatinx was called to the stage to receive their award from Equality Florida, members gathered to the stage, but not everyone could fit. Some folks stood on the stairs leading to the stage, squeezing together to fit into a picture for the photographer. As the photographer's camera shutter rapidly clicked, I stayed near the stage, applauding and whistling. Friends on stage turned and motioned for me to come up and join them, but I pointed out that there wasn't much room, and I wanted to be sure others had the ability to be photographed and recognized.

After the photo was taken, my husband approached me and said "everyone was asking why you didn't get on the stage. I told them you wouldn't, even if they asked." I asked him to explain what he meant, and he replied, "I know that you would want to save space for others, but you could have gone up there—you're still part of the organization."

In some ways, that exact point describes one element of how I view the work of accompaniment. For me, accompaniment includes membership in efforts to advance a particular political cause or work toward the shared goal of health equity, as well as a critical reflection of power, privilege, and positionality. As a cisgender white man without concerns over immigration status, I am often given literal and metaphorical stages upon which to stand and handed literal and metaphorical microphones while given the opportunity to speak first. To me, accompaniment includes an element of reflecting on such power and privilege and assuring that those with whom I work get a stage, microphone, spotlight, and space to stand or sit at the table—whether literal or metaphorical.

Like activist anthropologists, I see accompaniment work as including a deep commitment to a shared political goal. In the case of QLatinx, that shared political goal continues to be working toward justice for all people and emphasizing interlocking sources of oppression that create forms of marginalization and erasure for people at the intersection of multiple minoritized identities. To me, accompaniment squarely emphasizes social relationships over research or work-related relationships. It means being a member of a movement family and emphasizing the importance of the relationships with other members of the movement family. This work, then, often carries with it deep emotional connections and commitments.

Nicole Novak: A Bad Epidemiologist

When I first approached the Center for Worker Justice (CWJ) of Eastern Iowa, I was a graduate student who had returned to her hometown in Iowa for family caregiving reasons. I was excited to see that my home county, Johnson County, was planning to implement a Community ID card, and had begun to talk to the CWJ about the idea of a survey evaluation. In a stroke of fate, I learned that Alana and Bill (coauthors on this chapter) were about to implement a study in partnership with advocates at the Washtenaw ID Project in Ann Arbor, Michigan. The Washtenaw ID launched a month ahead of Johnson County's Community ID, and I began to work with and learn from the Washtenaw team.

Looking back, I think I was destined to take a path from mainstream social epidemiology to community-engaged research to a public health of accompaniment. Years earlier, I had immersed myself in the tradition of accompaniment as it was conceived in liberation theology, particularly in Central America. I had spent several years working with (and sometimes living in) Catholic worker communities that radically center the humanity and dignity of those who are pushed to the margins. However, I was still figuring out how to integrate those values into my work as a public health scholar.

I went back to my initial notes on the Community ID study, and they are so clearly informed by the ways I was being "disciplined" in social epidemiology. Having been trained to prioritize causal inference above all else, I described the ID policy as a potential "natural experiment" whereby groups of people in Johnson County would have access to a buffer against some immigration-related stressors, whereas people in other counties would not. I hypothesized that researchers could document reductions in stress through a difference-in-differences analysis comparing changes in counties with IDs to changes in counties without IDs.

I wanted to work closely with CWJ, but the ways I understood a research partnership were closer to a traditional community-academic partnership; I would make sure the study also answered CWJ's questions and helped them pursue resources or changes that were meaningful to them, and they could help build trust and encourage participation in the survey.

But the Washtenaw ID study was not about a "natural experiment" whereby people experiencing immigration-related stress were subjected to local policies. The organizers of the project centered the knowledge and priorities of the community groups that organized for the ID, and they committed to a tight intertwining of research and advocacy. In addition to collecting surveys, the study team offered bilingual support at the site of application. There was a fund to support people with the ID application fee, funded by donated research incentives from survey participants who were willing to share their incentive payment.

In Johnson County, I began to work closely with Sergio, CWJ's Community ID coordinator, to conduct a "sister study" with many similar features. We sat in the entry to the county administration building, wearing shirts that said, "Identify Me!" in each of CWJ's core languages: Spanish, French, and Arabic. We helped people with their applications and sometimes went to bat for them when the county staff were not familiar with the myriad reasons someone had atypical paperwork, such as only having a photocopy of a passport because the original was being held by Border Patrol. As someone trained in a wing of public health that was largely positivist, centered the "expertise" of researchers over community knowledge, and prioritized statistical sophistication over community trust and accountability, the project felt to me like coming home. After being in a field that made me wonder if my commitment to community would cast doubt on my "objectivity" as a scholar, or, more simply, make me a bad epidemiologist, it was so energizing to do work where caring for people was a strength, not a weakness or distraction. I was so proud on the day that our Johnson County research team paused survey data collection to step outside the county administration building and join CWJ in a protest to raise the Johnson County minimum wage.

By the end of data collection and during our first waves of dissemination, I would say this was a heartfully community-rooted study. In the years following, it moved toward accompaniment—a more intricate intertwining of lives and passions, work and play. I spent a lot of time at the center, learning about their campaigns and communities. Whereas academic public health, even community-engaged research or CBPR, incentivizes us to work in a linear, focused way, I saw more and more clearly that this was not how life challenges presented themselves to people in the community. The Community ID was sometimes a priority, and sometimes it wasn't.

For example, on the day we were planning to present the results of the Community ID study, several undergraduate and masters students had meticulously prepared to share a bilingual presentation at a monthly meeting of CWJ members. However, that meeting became an emergency response meeting because the owner of Rose Oaks, a local housing complex that was home to many low-income residents, had announced that it would not be renewing residents' leases, leaving many of them in a housing crisis. In contrast to hierarchical and structured academic spaces, CWJ's meeting needed to respond to urgent community needs. It didn't mean that the Community ID wasn't important, but on that day, it needed to wait.

By the time I moved back to Iowa City for a postdoctoral position at the University of Iowa College of Public Health, CWJ was just a part of my life. One of the parents wanted science activities for a summer children's program. A young father came in after missing work for his daughter's medical appointments led to him being fired from work at a swine inseminator. A woman was trying to get her cell phone back from local police after they confiscated it during an investigation of a robbery at the store where she worked. My husband and I made an activity about the water cycle. We joined a delegation to confront the manager at the swine inseminator. I drove the woman to the police station and interpreted her objections into English as the officers told her she had (technically) voluntarily given them her phone—she hadn't realized she was permitted to refuse. I listened to her. A neighbor who was a professor warned me against getting distracted from my postdoc. I heard what he was saying. I couldn't listen to him.

Walking with CWJ—and those I met through the organization—even when it wasn't directly related to my research, opened up friendships and fruitful connections for the benefit of public health.

Public health of accompaniment sometimes felt like "bad behavior" as a social scientist because I was not resisting the urge to let my life intertwine with community experiences. As someone whose racial, class, and citizenship privilege have protected me from many of the challenges CWJ members face, I sometimes felt confused and uncomfortable about what my role should be in academic spaces. I didn't want to speak for people, but I saw so many gaping holes in standard academic work. People's lives were complex, not easily reduced to variables in the ways that social epidemiologists do. I often struggled against my academic perfectionism in a piece of writing when I knew someone needed a ride to an ICE check-in or another clearly defined task that I could easily do. I'm still finding my way with these things. What I do know is that accompaniment, bearing witness, standing in solidarity, are goods in themselves.

They build human connections, they honor dignity, they build understanding in a world riven with divides.

Alana LeBrón: Zapato del Migrante

There's a *zapato (shoe)*, small, about two inches long, made of wrappers from snacks purchased at the immigrant detention commissary, that moves throughout my house. At first, it was a key chain. Now that the dental floss that attached the zapato to the key ring has weathered, it is a memento that my son finds interesting and moves about our house every now and then. It was gifted to me by young adult Central American twin sisters, whom my husband, Mike, and I accompanied with their mother and aunt after they were released from immigrant detention. After spending a night in a hotel after their late release from detention, they came with us to purchase some cosmetics, clothes, and snacks at Target in preparation for their journey to Arizona to live with their new sponsor.

As they browsed throughout Target, they seemed unbothered by the monitors fastened to their ankles. After loading up the car with the essentials that we bought, we found a quaint Salvadoran restaurant and enjoyed a table full of warm dishes as we connected—learning their family's migration journey, the conditions that spurred their migration, that their father and brothers were still in detention, and their hopes for what lay ahead in Arizona. Mike and I shared that we were relatively new to California, how we met, and what we liked or found odd about Orange County. We all discussed our disappointment in the immigration politics in which they were entangled. So many tears, and also a little laughter.

With about an hour left before their bus was scheduled to depart, we packed up the leftovers, knowing that they would be a good treat on the Greyhound ride from Orange County to Arizona. We carefully packed their new belongings in zippered grocery bags from our car, then headed over to the bus station. What I thought would be a quick drop-off at the bus station turned into a long afternoon of delays, seemingly endless waiting, lack of information, and frustration during the five hours that it took from their expected departure until they could finally board their delayed bus, just as the summer sun was starting to set. These themes, it seemed, were not new; they were mundane parts of the sisters' experience caravanning north to the United States, and then in detention, as they awaited processing and release, and now, as they awaited learning about the fate of their father and brothers.

Was this public health research? CBPR? CEnR? While this dilemma may have originally made me uncomfortable, I rarely deliberate this question anymore, mostly because it feels like there is limited space in public health to unpack and hold these experiences in relation to our research and our field more broadly. Did I conduct an interview or survey? No. Did we explicitly discuss key issues affecting Central American migrants' health and what we as a field can do to better understand or address these priorities? No. These are prevailing perceptions of what public health research and CBPR look like. Certainly, these processes are critical to CBPR in public health. And yet, where does our day together fit in models of public health research? Our day together was one of accompanying the twins and their family as they marked their transition from the cold and harsh conditions in immigrant detention to Arizona where they would stay with a family they had never met but who had the interests and means to sponsor them.

My agenda that day was not research in a classical sense. My agenda that day was to lessen the harshness of our immigration enforcement system and to affirm that we were glad they made it to the United States and hoped and prayed that they would realize their hopes to be reunited with the rest of their family and find peace and economic stability in the United States. In our day together, I also learned about their experiences with our harsh immigration system and bore witness to their joy in being reunited and out of detention.

What I can say is that this day touched me—as a researcher, an immigration advocate, a teacher, and a third-generation Boricua, who saw and felt moments of resonance with my grandparents' own challenges to settle and make a home on the mainland.

Conclusion

Accompaniment work, as the editors of this volume describe in the introduction, is "an ethical commitment, calling us as engaged or activist anthropologists to action, to take stances in the world in solidarity with those whose lives we seek to understand, to use our positions of relative privilege as resources for the amelioration of suffering." We view a public health of accompaniment similarly, as a calling to stand in solidarity with those whose lives we study, to embrace the emotions that come from the documentation of their suffering, and to use our emotions—as well as our resources and positions of privilege—to walk with them toward a mutual goal of health equity.

To fully embrace a public health of accompaniment, the field of public health, like anthropology, must have its own postmodern, humanistic turn, not only moving away from positivism but also fully embracing that advocacy and public health are inextricably linked. Positivists obsess over the false notion of the unbiased researcher and question immigration scholars' distance from the issues we study. Advocacy is seen as going beyond our roles as researchers, or classified simply as a form of service, rather than being an essential part of our work. While CBPR provides a framework for us as a field to confront the misguided concept of positivism and to instead elevate community knowledge, gatekeepers have latched onto a very narrow model of CBPR, often with limited attention to equity. Often, in this perceived application of CBPR, perhaps far from the original purpose of the model, grasstops are at the proverbial research table, yet not a table in which power may be fully shared. Often, in this common interpretation of CBPR, lacking in the research process are human connections to those most impacted by the inequitable systems we are trying to understand and transform.

A public health of accompaniment must also allow for relationships and support that extend beyond research goals and outcomes. So many of us have been socialized to believe that personal relationships distract from the objectivity we need for research, or, worse, that offering other assistance besides that of the intervention will muddle the clarity of the intervention's success. But we often felt it impossible not to get involved with people's lives when they needed assistance we could provide, from health programs with their kids to the many, many rides we have given over the past ten years. As public health professionals who care deeply about those with whom we work—and who feel rage and grief when they suffer—how could we not?

To engage in a public health of accompaniment, public health professionals must also reckon with our need to be efficient and productive.

Accompaniment work can be slow, boring, mundane, and extremely inefficient. Unlike academic work, which prioritizes productivity efficiency, and control of one's schedule, accompaniment work can be random, unpredictable, and, sometimes, unsuccessful, or at least have no clear outcome. This again underscores the tensions between classic CBPR and CEnR perspectives and what we know and feel is accompaniment work in public health. More than completed surveys or a day of data collection, accompaniment work is about holding true to commitments to both individuals and movements, which often means including our families. While we may be skilled researchers, that's not always what matters. We also provide rides to Target for clothing, complete a spreadsheet to organize volunteers, or invite a family over for a warm meal and some other kids to play with. We see each of these as work toward dismantling harsh and unjust systems, such as the immigration system.

As we have shown in this collection of essays, a public health of accompaniment is not a merger of research and service, nor is it driven by positivist obsession. Rather, this work is about combating the deeply rooted systems of harm that hurt people and communities we care about deeply, using our privileges to engage in the "micro-advocacy," mentioned by Horton in chapter 4 of this volume, that benefits the people in our lives who happen to be part of our research interests, and doing so despite what conventional academic wisdom might suggest. The combination of using research as a tool for social justice, being aware of our privileges and resources available to us so that we can use them in our accompaniment work and honoring the individuals in our work first and foremost, form the core of public health of accompaniment.

References

Abrego, Lesley J., and Cecilia Menjívar. 2011. "Immigrant Latina Mothers as Targets of Legal Violence." *International Journal of Sociology of the Family* 37 (1): 9–26.

Alonso, Jorge. 2009. "Zapatistas Organize the First Global Festival of Dignified Rage." *Envío. Informacion sobre Nicaragua y Centroamerica* 330.

Behar, Ruth. 1996. *The Vulnerable Observer: Anthropology That Breaks Your Heart.* Boston, MA: Beacon Press.

Behar, Ruth. 2012. "What Renato Rosaldo Gave Us." *Aztlan: A Journal of Chicano Studies* 37 (1): 205–211.

Collins, Katherine M., Nicole L. Novak, Gladys E. Godinez, Tamera L. Shull, and William D. Lopez. 2022. "The Repercussions of Large-Scale Immigration Worksite Raids on Immigrant Women: Results from Six Rural Communities." *Journal of Community Practice* 30 (2): 128–142.

Dunn, Linda. 1991. "Research Alert! Qualitative Research May Be Hazardous to Your Health." *Qualitative Health Research* 1 (3): 388–392.

Hale, Charles R. 2006. "Activist Research v. Cultural Critique: Indigenous Land Rights and the Contradictions of Politically Engaged Anthropology." *Cultural Anthropology* 21 (1): 96–120.

Israel, Barbara A., Amy J. Schulz, Edith A. Parker, Adam B. Becker, Alex J. Allen, Ricardo Guzman, and R. Lichtenstein. 2017. "Critical Issues in Developing and Following CBPR Principles." *Community Based Participatory Research for Health: Advancing Social and Health Equity* 3: 32–35.

Kline, Nolan. 2018. *Pathogenic Policing: Immigration Enforcement and Health in the U.S. South*. New Brunswick, NJ: Rutgers University Press.

Krieger, N. 1999. "Questioning Epidemiology: Objectivity, Advocacy, and Socially Responsible Science." *American Journal of Public Health* 89 (8): 1151–1153.

LeBrón, Alana M. W., Keta Cowan, William D. Lopez, Nicole L. Novak, Maria Ibarra-Frayre, and Jorge Delva. 2019. "The Washtenaw ID Project: A Government-Issued ID Coalition Working toward Social, Economic, and Racial Justice and Health Equity." *Health Education and Behavior* 46 (1S): 53S–61S.

LeBrón, Alana M. W., William D. Lopez, K. Cowan, Nicole L. Novak, O. Temrowski, M. Ibarra-Frayre, and J. Delva. 2018. "Restrictive ID Policies: Implications for Health Equity." *Journal of Immigrant and Minority Health* 20 (2): 255–260.

Lopez, William D. 2019. *Separated: Family and Community in the Aftermath of an Immigration Raid*. Baltimore, MD: Johns Hopkins University Press.

Lopez, William D., and Heide Castañeda. 2022. "The Mixed-Status Community as Analytic Framework to Understand the Impacts of Immigration Enforcement on Health." *Social Science and Medicine* 307 (August). https://doi.org/10.1016/j.socscimed.2022.115180.

Lopez, William D., Katherine M. Collins, Guadalupe R. Cervantes, Dalila Reynosa, Julio C. Salazar, and Nicole L. Novak. 2022. "Large-Scale Immigration Worksite Raids and Mixed-Status Families: Separation, Financial Crisis, and Family Role Rearrangement." Family and Community Health 45 (2): 59–66. https://doi.org/10.1097/FCH.0000000000000322.

Lopez, William D., Daniel J. Kruger, Jorge Delva, Mikel Llanes, Charo Ledón, Adreanne Waller, Melanie Harner, et al. 2017. "Health Implications of an Immigration Raid: Findings from a Latino Community in the Midwestern United States." *Journal of Immigrant and Minority Health* 19 (3): 702–708.

Lopez, William D., Nicole L. Novak, Melanie Harner, Ramiro Martinez, and Julia S. Seng. 2018. "The Traumatogenic Potential of Law Enforcement Home Raids: An Exploratory Report." *Journal of Traumatology* 24 (3): 193–199.

Luger, Tana M., Alison B. Hamilton, and Gala True. 2020. "Measuring Community-Engaged Research Contexts, Processes, and Outcomes, a Mapping Review." *The Milbank Quarterly* 98 (2): 493–553.

Novak, Nicole L., Arline T. Geronimus, and Aresha M. Martinez-Cardoso. 2017. "Change in Birth Outcomes among Infants Born to Latina Mothers after a Major Immigration Raid." *International Journal of Epidemiology* 46 (3): 839–849.

Petillo, April. 2020. "Unsettling Ourselves: Notes on Reflective Listening beyond Discomfort." *Feminist Anthropology* 1 (1): 14–23.

Rager, Kathleen B. 2005. "Compassion Stress and the Qualitative Researcher." *Qualitative Health Research* 3:423–430.

Rosaldo, Renato. 2004. "Grief and a Headhunter's Rage." In *Death, Mourning, and Burial: A Cross-Cultural Reader*, edited by Antonius C. G. M. Robben, 167–178. Oxford and Malden, MA: Blackwell Publishing.

Rosas, Gilberto. 2021. "Grief and Border-Crossing Rage." *Anthropology and Humanism* 46 (1): 114–128.

Smith, Erin, Julie-Ann Pooley, Lisa Homes, Kristine Gebbie, and Robyn Gershon. 2021. "Vicarious Trauma: Exploring the Experiences of Qualitative Researchers Who Study Traumatized Populations." *Disaster Medicine and Public Health Preparedness* 17, no. 1 (e69).

Speed, Shannon. 2006. "At the Crossroads of Human Rights and Anthropology: Towards a Critically Engaged Activist Research." *American Anthropologist* 108 (1): 66–76.

Thangadurai, P., and K. S. Jacob. 2014. "Medicalizing Distress, Ignoring Public Health Strategies." *Indian Journal of Psychological Medicine* 36 (4): 351–354.

Wallerstein, Nina, and Bonnie Duran. 2017. "Theoretical, Historical, and Practice Roots of CBPR." In *Community-Based Participatory Research for Health: Advancing Social and Health Equity*, 3rd ed., edited by Nina Wallerstein, Bonnie Duran, John G. Oetzel, and Meredith Minkler, 17–29. San Francisco: Jossey-Bass.

CHAPTER 7

Accompaniment and Testimonio

Migration Narratives in and beyond the U.S.-Mexico Borderlands

TOBIN HANSEN AND MARÍA ENGRACIA ROBLES ROBLES

Accompaniment entails being present together, intertwining lives to provide reciprocal support and draw collective purpose (see Yarris and Duncan in the introduction). Co-presence is often understood as inhabiting place together: being with others and experiencing the world together. Might accompaniment exist, however, with and through *testimonio*—first-person narrative accounts—despite physical distance or absence? Are there ways of "being-with," as Kristin Yarris and Whitney Duncan frame the concept in the introduction to this volume, available when people have moved on, but narrative texts and memories remain? We suggest that telling, listening, documenting, holding, and circulating testimonios enable a form of accompaniment, of being present and in solidarity with others even when we're geographically separated. After testimonio is given and recorded, it becomes present in us who have given it or heard or read it. Moreover, its traces live on beyond recorded or textual forms, accompanying and implicating us in shared social and political struggles.

In this chapter, we examine how accompaniment emerges in both physical presence and absences, persists through the sharing of testimonios, and circulates between vulnerable people and others who stand in solidarity. To provide insight, we draw from our work in Nogales, Sonora, Mexico, on the northern Mexico border. We recount our experiences side-by-side in everyday spaces with people on the move or stuck in place, as well as our project of collecting testimonios and envisioning, crafting, and presenting a co-edited book of first-person narratives of being called *Voices of the Border: Testimonios of Migration, Deportation, and Asylum* (Hansen and Robles 2021), published in 2021 by Georgetown University Press. The purpose of the volume is to raise awareness of migration and border issues among students—at advanced high school, undergraduate, and graduate levels—as well as researchers, teachers, and other community members. As a publicly engaged scholar from the United States, in Tobin's case, and a grassroots educator from Mexico, in the case of Engracia, we have realized that our approaches to community-engaged learning and producing knowledge are not so different. The co-presence we have sought to nurture—reflected in our ongoing work and relationships with migrants, asylum seekers, and deported people as well as with each other—is affective, material, and embodied. Moreover, textual forms of co-presence, which we examine in this chapter based on our experience producing and presenting *Voices,* offer possibilities for accompaniment through the production, circulations, and afterlives of first-person narratives.

In what follows, we describe the book project generally, examine testimonio as both a political and intimate human act, and each share how we came to envision accompaniment as a part of our work. We then examine linkages between testimonio and accompaniment and conclude by offering final insights into accompaniment and the liberatory power of testimonio.

Before continuing, however, an explanation of our conjoined efforts to write this chapter offers perspective on the forms that our accompaniment of one another has taken. We met over Zoom sessions—Engracia from Nogales, Sonora, and Tobin from Lebanon, Oregon—imagining together what a chapter might contribute. We talked one another into the challenge of drafting a reflective chapter that, we hoped, might recast the relationships between testimonio and accompaniment as well as reaffirm the importance of alliances that cross boundaries of nation, race, language, religion, intellectual traditions, and vocation to "[enrich] both process and outcome, given the multiple eyes, brains, hearts, and experiences that can be dedicated to research problems and questions" (Staudt 2013, 54). We muddled our way to some directions for the text, eventually committing to deadlines for draft sections we would each write and share in Spanish with one another and then discuss, improve, edit, and rewrite. Tobin translated the draft to English, sharpened the prose, and retooled sections to ensure that both of our voices came through—using "we" throughout the chapter, save for the more personalized third and fourth sections, where we each use "I"—to communicate one message. We actively deferred to one another during the project, asking questions about the other's perspective, and arrived at consensus regarding the chapter's structure and key arguments. In the process, we exchanged emails with peppy exclamation points and, over Zoom, rehashed memories, shared laughs, and commiserated about borderlands hardships. And we rolled up our sleeves and got to work.

Testimonio, Accompaniment, and *Voices of the Border*

The Spanish verb forms *ofrecer testimonio, testificar,* or *atestiguar* convey subtleties: emphasizing the giving or transmission of narrative, or the act of legitimating truth claims and affirming their evidentiary value. These nuances reflect two important valences of testimonio in the context of human displacement, movement, and confinement. First, those who provide testimonio embody the role of declarations-giver—they become witnesses. Second, they become experts whose explanations hold weight (Stephen 2013, 8–13). Once people who migrate, are deported, or seek asylum become legible as witnesses whose insights reflect critical aspects of migratory political economies and migration experiences, the potential emerges for marginalized people on the move or stuck in place—devalued in popular discourse—to "become seen as authentic, proper, and warranted participants in history as well as makers of history" (Hansen 2021, 5). Moreover, as a witness to one's own experience, the recounting of testimonio repositions migrants within competing narratives of migrants-as-victims, migrants-as-lawbreakers, and migrants-as-social-problem (Yarris 2022, 175–176). Giving testimonio, then, constitutes a legitimating act as well as a political one, insofar as it holds some possibility for shaping perceptions and effectuating change in the medium or long term (Stephen 2017). Sharing testimonio at once permits expressions of intimate, individual lifeworlds and enables reflection of lives subjected to the blunt force of inequities in interlocking social, economic, and political structures (Lusk and Villalobos 2012; Stephen 2017; Tula and Stephen 1994). Testimonio is different from interviewing.

Whereas interviews are often driven by what interviewers want to know and subjected to interviewers' analysis, testimonio seeks to shift power imbalances by emphasizing the validity of testimonio givers in providing lengthy, less directed accounts. Testimonio informs notions of collective life and has the potential to raise visibility for larger projects related to justice, coexistence with others, and the reaffirmation of people's dignity and inherent worth (Stephen 2013).

Testimonio enables accompaniment. As a fundamental act of sharing, storytelling is constitutive of reciprocal human enmeshments. As Vargas, López, and Duncan put it in their chapter in this volume, *convivencia* is a way of being together that both materializes from and produces storytelling and testimonio as we share struggles and life's mundanities. Narratives of discrepancies between, on the one hand, expectations of opportunities to achieve a modest standard of wellbeing and, on the other, life's everyday disarray, give insight into how "life problems are created, controlled, and made meaningful" (Kleinman 1988, xiii; see also Kleinman 2007). Within contexts of pain and suffering—such as being stuck in northern Mexico far from home and family, living traumas of displacement with little hope for legal avenues to refuge—stories facilitate understandings of hardship (Kleinman 2007). As stories of experiences are shared, their potential for elucidating shared humanity and creating empathic responses may resituate people within relational status hierarchies, facilitating empowerment (Ralph 2014, 129–130) and, we suggest, accompaniment. Testimonio, as a form of narrative exchange, reflects a desire to listen, understand, and take seriously. Storytelling becomes existential, in implicating entwined interpersonal, moral lives and in making and remaking the fluid boundaries that inscribe the self and others in mutual, ongoing projects of personhood (Han 2012, 17; see also Kleinman 2007; Ralph 2014).

Voices is the fruit of collaborative labor whose cultivation has enabled various forms of physical and textual co-presence. It comprises eleven thematic chapters, each introduced with a brief contextualizing essay written by a Mexican or American academic or humanitarian aid worker. At its heart are thirty-seven testimonios,[1] curated from hundreds that

1. We anonymized the names of people and places and changed other identifying details for the safety of those who gave testimonios.

Engracia has collected, given by people on the move, expelled by the U.S. government or wishing to find refuge, who have come to stay or pass through Nogales, Mexico, a node situated within unequal capitalist and statist structures and through which, over years, millions of people have passed (Hansen 2021, xi). As a nun working in Nogales, Mexico since 2007, Engracia has carried out humanitarian aid and educational work with people who migrate, are deported, or seek asylum. She invited people to share their stories, to be recorded and disseminated without knowing until conceiving of the *Voices* project years later that they would be compiled in a book. Tobin joined the project in 2017, while conducting dissertation research in cultural anthropology that he undertook in 2013 with men deported from the United States to Nogales. Tobin shepherded the text of *Voices*; curating testimonios, writing contextualizing chapter introductions, and editing introductory contributions from a group of migrant advocate collaborators. The work we both have done with people in situations of mobility and forcible immobility reflects a desire to open small spaces to intimacy and sharing that reflect an appreciation for others' humanity. Moreover, book presentations we have given together and separately have catalyzed conversations around migration justice with university faculty, students, and other justice advocates.

Engracia's Pathway to Accompaniment, Testimonio, *and* Voices

In 2007, I started working with people deported to Nogales, Sonora, Mexico by happenstance. I needed to channel my humanitarian impulse. As a young nun in the early 1960s, I had been deeply motivated by the Second Vatican Council and the notion that Christian belief ought to motivate support for marginalized people in service of a more just world (O'Malley 2008). This feeling was cemented in 1987–1988, when I was working in Brazil and studying liberation theology—a Christian theology that emphasizes the liberation of people relegated to the social, economic, and political margins. In early 2007, I was guiding younger members in my religious order, in a formation house in Guadalajara dedicated to the study of philosophy. There I realized that I was too steeped in an inward-looking religious culture that was overly concerned with its leaders and institutions, forgetting a world around it composed of people struggling for survival. In 2007, the Jesuit Refugee Service (JRS) wanted to know the needs of migrants and deportees in Nogales in order to develop an infrastructure of support. I went to Nogales to gather information on JRS's behalf. I hoped that a new work focus, in Nogales, would free me from that self-centered whirlpool.

I was completely unfamiliar with the nuances of migration, especially in the U.S.-Mexico border context. The volume of deportations in Nogales was particularly high in 2007. In August alone a total of 7,402 people were deported to Nogales, 20 percent of whom were women (SEGOB/INM 2011, 97–98). It was easy for me to get in touch with them since all day every day U.S. government agents emptied trucks of deported migrants on the Arizona side of the border. People crossed into Mexico hungry, afraid, and at risk. Bodily trauma was readily apparent, as in the sores on the soles of their feet from walking in the desert. We offered them something to eat and talked right there on the side of the road. I was surprised at how many non-migrants interacted with them upon arrival—human smugglers (called *coyotes*), extortionists, kidnappers, everyday workers, taxi drivers, and others—to the benefit and detriment of deported people. Developing a clinical eye for identifying risks became my first great challenge. My eyes had been opened to the knowledge that migration created opportunities for abuse and crime.

In 2008, we set up a small shelter for migrant women and a *comedor*, or dining room, for all, just a few hundred yards south of the U.S-Mexico border.[2] The work brought me closer to migrants. I began to listen to stories, especially with women in the shelter. A community formed, characterized by sharing and trust. Women saw their pain and frustration in one another—they had no reason to hide it—and spoke frankly with each other. Some had just been deported upon attempting entry to the United States for work, tired of being exploited for low wages in Mexico, and were realizing the dissolution of their dreams. Others spoke of other motivations for migration, such as domestic and gender-based violence. Some recounted the hunger, cold, fatigue, loneliness, and suffering of the desert. Abusive *coyotes* had deceived, cheated, and even raped some of

2. This would eventually become the Kino Border Initiative, which provides direct humanitarian aid, advocates to policy-makers, and offers educational opportunities related to migration justice.

them; some had been abandoned in the desert. Others arrived with their feet flayed. Some people recounted hardship in Nogales after deportation: robberies, extortion, and threats from the mafia. Others emphasized the intrafamilial violence from which they were fleeing or abuses by government agents who took advantage of their trip to extort them. The most heartbroken, however, were those who had been separated from their children—Mexican national adults deported to Mexico with U.S. citizen children who had remained in the United States. The outlook was bleak.

In the midst of all this, I wondered: What happens with all this suffering, all the stories people have and share? Who takes account of them? Why are there so many people who seem like they were born to suffer? And if the migrants to whom I listened seemed like heroes, why so much discrimination, violence, prejudice, rejection, and xenophobia toward them? I realized the power that such testimonios had because of what they produced in me. I was left feeling awe-struck, at times powerless, and an overwhelming goodwill and desire to commit my support. Their experiences seemed sacred, worthy of being documented, published, well-known, and even revered—not ignored and buried in oblivion. Perhaps these testimonios could exert a change in immigration policies. On the other hand, if I collected testimonios, what would I do with them? What would be the purpose of archiving or storing them? How might they be brought to light? I didn't know. The value of the stories, however, left me feeling that they needed to be collected.

The power of testimonios became clear to me as I sent them out to religious communities, convents, and churches so that at least the sisters who are dedicated to praying would have people to pray for. In churches in Nogales, Sonora, they brought home everyday realities of the community outside the church walls, confronting the people inside with the demands of the gospel. I also started to raise awareness on the radio, encouraging listeners to welcome migrants and revere the courage and strength implied by risking one's life for the good of themself and their family. Simultaneous to my promoting these narratives, other versions spread about migrants. According to Trump's racist stereotypes about migrants, "They're bringing drugs. They're bringing crime. They're rapists" (Washington Post Staff 2015). I knew the opposite. I saw brave people who sacrificed for love of family—taking risks, including the risk of death, and leaving behind any semblance of comfort to cross into the United States and achieve a dignified life for loved ones.

Accompaniment through storytelling reflected the value of social and political equities espoused during the Second Vatican Council and a liberation theology which, since the 1980s, has been particularly resonant in Latin America. Subsequently, the Church has reoriented its praxis away from abstract, decontextualized ritualism and toward a God who exists in the world. This reorientation seeks freedom for oppressed and marginalized people as well as the engagement of all people in pursuing justice in the world. Producing testimonios, accordingly, at once renders visible social injustices and highlights the need for social and political change while also opening spaces for meaningful interaction between givers and documenters of testimonio as well as between testimonio in textual form and those who come to read it.

This theological grounding, which informed my engagement with migrants and people deported or seeking asylum, fueled the desire to publish a book, a distant but clear dream. That desire was like a seed being saved with no conditions to germinate, but with all its potential to grow and bloom. When I had collected hundreds of testimonios to put together the chapters of a book, I needed great collaborators. I wanted to find people who could perceive beyond what can be seen with the naked eye, who would call things by their name, who would not justify what happens as normal, who were objective in the face of the realities of injustice. In other words, I wanted to find people who are critical of the system who, with wisdom and thoughtfulness, would see these testimonies for what they are: the consequence of an unfair and inhumane system.

During that period of looking for collaborators, I met Tobin in 2014 on a trip from Nogales to El Paso, organized by my co-worker and friend Marla Conrad. I didn't know Tobin and, when Marla said she wanted to catch up on sleep in the back of the car and leave Tobin and me up front, I couldn't help but fixate on the stereotype that all anthropologists are atheists. I wondered: What are an atheist anthropologist and a nun going to talk about, stuck together in a car for eight long hours? Surprisingly, it was an eye-opening trip: I learned a lot about Tobin; his friendship with Latinx people since his childhood as a white, non-Latinx person; his youth in Guadalajara; his college teaching; his solidarity with Mexican people. He seemed like the ideal person: straightforward, critical and thoughtful, and prepared as a scholar. He told me he wanted to give back to the community for the support he was receiving while doing research. Those words filled me with hope. He was busy then. In 2017, when he finished his dissertation fieldwork, he committed to the project that would become *Voices*. My dream came true.

Tobin's Pathway to Collaboration

I became an anthropologist to make aspects of human life, particularly in Latin America and Mexico, more visible to people in the United States. Further, anthropology provides useful perspective given my personal and political commitments to migration justice, which originated with social and activist solidarity with transnational Latinx communities in Oregon, where I am from, and central Pacific Mexico. These commitments were strengthened in Nogales, Sonora, Mexico, after an invitation in July 2013 to spend time with and increase the visibility of a small community of deported men. The invitation came on a car trip from Oregon to west Texas to conduct summer research as a graduate student, when I decided to take extra time and detour south from Tucson, Arizona, to visit Nogales, a border town I had never seen. Walking on a narrow street south of the tourist area that abuts the U.S.-Mexico boundary in the blistering late morning, I saw two men sitting on the sidewalk ahead of me. Oscar[3]—with prominent tattoos, shaved head, and tight tank top—hustled up to me in hopes, I would later learn, that I would lend him some money. He and Miguel, who had both lived several decades in Phoenix and Los Angeles, respectively, told me about living in the United States for decades, since childhood, being incarcerated in U.S. prisons, and experiencing the hardships of a deportation that wasn't a return home but a banishment from home. Upon learning that I was doing anthropological research, Oscar said, "Write about us." I listened intently as he talked about the

3. Real name. In the years Tobin spent close to Oscar, from meeting him in July 2013 until he died in June 2017, he wanted Tobin to use his real name when writing about his life. He agreed to a pseudonym, Danny, while he was alive, when Tobin proposed the idea. Over the years he would jokingly refer to himself as Danny, for example when Tobin visited him in his small cement house: "Hey Tobin, how's it going? Checking in to see how ol' Danny is doing . . ."

need to raise awareness about the U.S. government's deportation apparatus as an act of solidarity, saying that deportees were the "trash the United States takes out" and that "we're the forgotten people." Oscar and Miguel said that there were lots of deported people around and that I should listen to what they had to say and get the word out. Oscar became a collaborator and a friend who always envisioned publications influencing U.S. public opinion, despite my efforts to dampen his illusions. Multiple traumas and health problems contributed to his death on June 11, 2017. Oscar is one of several deported people I have lived with closely over the years, although not the only one who has died in Mexico. *Que en paz descansen.* Their stories live on.

An opportunity to recount narratives of being stuck in northern Mexico came in 2017, when Engracia and I entered into a formal collaboration to put a collection of testimonios together in readable form. We began the process of curating, and I provided context by writing and editing short chapter introductions. Engracia's invitation to collaborate—a few years earlier when I had just begun dissertation research with Oscar, Miguel, and others—incited acute emotions. Engracia's dedication to collecting personal narratives reflected deep commitment, clear vision, and tenacity. Her decades of experience working with marginalized communities afforded her clarity of insight, wisdom, patience, tirelessness, and grace. And I loved spending time with her.

The collaboration has been invigorating and wholly gratifying. Eventually, I came to see the project as analytically robust not despite but because of its ground-up, community-based, non-academic origin. Engracia's attentiveness to people's own accounting for their lives, circumstances, choices, and perceptions permitted granular understanding of migration and border dynamics. Her consideration of people's affective states and material and emotional needs within the rhythms and cultural expectations of the *comedor* cultivated an ethos of support and respect. This trumped concern with anthropological theories of human culture and disciplinary practices surrounding research populations, sampling, interviewing, or spatial or residential mapping, although her insights are always clear and her analysis sharp. More broadly, I saw Engracia's work and our collaboration as part of a larger movement of challenging the colonial hierarchies embedded in practices of knowledge production (Heyman 2013; Lassiter 2005). In other words, I have come to experience the project as an important response to calls to "decolonize ethnographic research—to reexamine its history, reinvent its present, and reimagine its future" (Alonso Bejarano et al. 2019, 7).

Engracia's conscientiousness in relating to those around her is echoed in the reciprocity and mutual support I sought with deported men in Nogales who participated in my dissertation research. Our disparate social locations—produced by race, ethnicity, class, and citizenship—structured our differing access to lucrative work, movement across the U.S.-Mexico border, and concomitant opportunities to physically accompany loved ones in the United States. In response to the power disparities between my interlocutors and myself, I have actively sought accountability to them through attentiveness to opportunities to be co-present, to listen and share what I have: time, money, food, clothing, my cell phone, information, and my humanity. I have also accompanied in the embodied sense, to doctor, attorney, and government appointments; to meet family; spend holidays together; and regularly visit Oscar and other deported people spending time in residential drug rehabilitation centers. Moreover, I have shaped research questions and analyses through conscientious, often impromptu, collaboration and continual dialogue about ways of making their struggle visible.

Accompaniment and Amplifying Voices

As we've considered the interpersonal ethics of our work on *Voices*, beyond the potential for any educational or political impact, we often ask: Is this accompaniment? And if so, in what ways? For years we have questioned the meanings and consequences of our relationships with those who give testimonio. We've gotten a sense of people's feelings about telling their story—from cynicism about any possibility that testimonios will have an influence, to indifference, to a sense of activist solidarity, to effusive enthusiasm. Migration activists, scholars, and readers have given us direct feedback as well, when we have given book presentations to student groups, classes, and civic organizations in the United States and Mexico since *Voices* was published in 2021. We've heard people's admiration for a book that reproduces affecting and experience-near narratives while illuminating historical and structural social, economic, and political aspects of immigration restrictionism.

Despite the appreciation, we both have doubted that the work that produced *Voices* comprises a form of accompaniment. The "doing with" of accompaniment as navigation and accompaniment as partnership in action that Sarah Horton describes in chapter 4 that highlights her relationships with Amparo and Elisa appears to contrast with our experiences with migrants and deported people. We, Tobin and Engracia, often share experiences with people on the move or stuck—interacting, sharing moments, finding commonality—to then realize after days or weeks or, sometimes, months or years, that a person has to move on or has moved on from Nogales. We feel co-presence and the entanglements of reciprocal support for a time, but for many, Nogales is a place to pass through and not a final destination. People get stuck, newly deported south with nowhere to go or recently arrived north and stopped by a border fence and guards and a U.S. government asylum and immigration regime that doesn't admit people like them. And, after some time, they are on the move again. Sometimes togetherness ends abruptly—other times, it gently dissipates. In a few cases, Engracia has sustained relationships; for example, with people who have stayed at the women's shelter, who have called, been in touch over Facebook, or been back to Nogales. And Tobin has been able to maintain contact—over Facebook, WhatsApp, telephone calls, and periodic visits from Oregon—and "do with," with several deported people he has met in Nogales since 2013. Other times, however, we don't know where people we were once close to have ended up or how they are. We're reminded of this by readers of *Voices*. During most book presentations we are asked: Where are they now? Where did Nayeli end up? What is Yésica doing? Where is Javier? Usually, we don't have an answer. We are left to imagine a person's struggles based on our experiences witnessing cycles of crossing attempts, deportations, or dealings with the U.S. government asylum apparatus. We can speculate about the next steps of someone's journey. But we often never find out. Our physical co-presence with people on the move or stuck in place is ephemeral.

We have come to understand, however, that accompaniment takes various forms. For one, we as collaborators have accompanied one another. The two of us have connected over our differing experiences living with people in extreme vulnerability, hardship, and abjection and related to it directly. We occasionally feel viscerally, in a surge of emotion, its effects on the lives of community members. At other times, everyday pressures demand attention, going here or there to do this or that: getting phone cards, helping fill out a form, grading student papers, getting to a meeting. These shared experiences, despite such disparate backgrounds and trajectories, provide commonality, as do our shared values surrounding migration equity, collaboration, education, and solidarity. All of that leads us to sense acutely in each other the support, camaraderie, strong friendship, and obligation that permit us to carry out the shared vision that we had committed to together. The trust and reliance on each other's judgement created shared stakes for *Voices*. Accompaniment has also sprung from our complementarity. Engracia had fostered trusting interactions and dedicated herself to sitting down and documenting difficult stories from a diverse group of people. Tobin was able to elicit a thick description of Engracia's vision for the project and brought his own scholarly expertise and descriptions of broad structures of inequality. We have worked long hours together, and separately, to meet objectives and deadlines and fulfill commitments to one another.

Circulating testimonio, after moments of physical proximity and co-presence have passed, likewise opens possibilities for accompaniment. The reading and rereading, sharing, and otherwise making available of testimonio—which motivates our book presentations, invited talks, and teaching and, we hope, occurs far beyond us—is a form of accompaniment in the shared struggle for migration justice. Such action enmeshes the everyday embodied struggles of people facing immigration restrictionism with our efforts to increase visibility and effect change. Here, Stephen's notion of "collaborative activist research" is instructive. Stephen understands it as a means by which researchers align themselves with community members and draw attention to shared stakes in political outcomes (Stephen 2021, 23). Aligning our efforts with those of migrants to raise awareness through testimonio—albeit from vastly different positions of privilege and oppression—then becomes its own form of collaboration, even beyond the temporal horizons of physical co-presence. Testimonio, part of the historical record of the consequences of immigration restrictionism, lives on in vibrant color and textured emotion, and bears witness to past vulnerabilities that migration systems have wrought and, moreover, presages the perpetuation of vulnerability if change isn't undertaken. For as long as they circulate and are remembered, narratives' afterlives persist. The accompaniment that materializes in shared struggle likewise lives on. As narratives circulate, accompaniment does as well. Stories are told and retold here and there, and accompaniment becomes multiple and circulates multidirectionally, transcending physical presence. As we accompany mobile and immobile people, they and their testimonios accompany us and other readers of testimonio.

Conclusions

The people we work with—who migrate, are deported, and seek asylum—and, frankly, most people in the global south and those who are marginalized in the global north, require radical change for the chance to flourish: change to labor and fiscal laws and regulations that, currently, exacerbate wealth inequality; to environmental laws that today are insufficient for reducing climate change; to health care laws that provide meager preventative and responsive medical services; and, of course, to freedom of movement that would enable relocation to communities with greater opportunities for well-being. A radical reenvisioning of the historical and contemporary inequities wrought by colonialism complements the everyday work to incrementally improve conditions at the margins, including through modest publications, like *Voices*, which pursue the aim of *concientización*, consciousness-raising.

The most important insights we have gained surround the limits of our interpersonal, co-present accompaniment and the power of testimonio to transcend those limitations. Testimonios accompany the two of us as writers and storytellers. They accompany others who permit themselves to be moved by stories they hear, read, and witness. We physically and affectively accompany—people on the move or stuck, as well as one another—in valuable yet limited and contingent ways, which eventually become disrupted by the vicissitudes of life. In their multidirectional movements, however, testimonios gain, rather than lose, their powers to describe, contextualize, reflect, emote, self-express, and participate in the struggle for migration justice. The impact of testimonios is revealed in those who hear them and is made visible in solidarity work such as direct aid, advocacy, activism, and education. Testimonios gain in their power to accompany as people process, question, and assimilate new perspectives into their worldview and come to share in the struggle.

References

Alonso Bejarano, Carolina, Lucia López Juárez, Mirian A. Mijangos, and Daniel M. Goldstien. 2019. *Decolonizing Ethnography: Undocumented Immigrants and New Directions in Social Science*. Durham, NC: Duke University Press.

Han, Clara. 2012. *Life in Debt: Times of Care and Violence in Neoliberal Chile*. Berkeley: University of California Press.

Hansen, Tobin. 2021. "Testimonios from Nogales." In *Voices of the Border: Testimonios of Migration, Deportation, and Asylum*, edited by Tobin Hansen and María Engracia Robles Robles, 1–21. Washington, D.C.: Georgetown University Press.

Hansen, Tobin, and María Engracia Robles Robles, eds. 2021. *Voices of the Border: Testimonios of Migration, Deportation, and Asylum*. Washington, D.C.: Georgetown University Press.

Heyman, Josiah McC. 2013. "Political-Ethical Dilemmas Participant Observed." In *Public Anthropology in a Borderless World*, edited by Sam Beck and Carl A. Maida, 118–143. New York: Berghahn.

Kleinman, Arthur. 1988. *The Illness Narratives: Suffering, Healing, and the Human Condition*. New York: Basic Books.

Kleinman, Arthur. 2007. *What Really Matters: Living a Moral Life amidst Uncertainty and Danger*. New York: Oxford University Press.

Lassiter, Luke Eric. 2005. *The Chicago Guide to Collaborative Anthropology*. Chicago: University of Chicago Press.

Lusk, Mark, and Griselda Villalobos. 2012. "The *Testimonio* of Eva: A Mexican Refugee in El Paso." *Journal of Borderlands Studies 27* (1): 17–25.

O'Malley, John W. 2008. *What Happened at Vatican II*. Cambridge, MA: Belknap Press of Harvard University Press.

Ralph, Laurence. 2014. *Renegade Dreams: Living through Injury in Gangland Chicago*. Chicago: University of Chicago Press.

Secretaría de Gobernación, Instituto Nacional de Migración. 2011. *Boletín mensual de estadísticas migratorias 2007*. Mexico City Centro de Estudios Migratorios.

Staudt, Kathleen. 2013. "The Good, the Bad, and the Ugly: Border Research Collaboration." In *Uncharted Terrains: New Directions in Border Research Methodology, Ethics, and Practice*, edited by Anna Ochoa O'Leary, Colin M. Deeds, and Scott Whiteford, 53–68. Tucson: University of Arizona Press.

Stephen, Lynn. 2013. *We Are the Face of Oaxaca: Testimony and Social Movements*. Durham, NC: Duke University Press.

Stephen, Lynn. 2017. "Bearing Witness: Testimony in Latin American Anthropology and Related Fields." *Journal of Latin American and Caribbean Anthropology* 22 (1): 85–109.

Stephen, Lynn. 2021. *Stories That Make History: Mexico through Elena Poniatowska's Crónicas*. Durham, NC: Duke University Press.

Tula, María Teresa, and Lynn Stephen. 1994. *Este es mi testimonio: María Teresa Tula, luchadora pro-derechos humanos de El Salvador [This is my testimonio:*

María Teresa Tula, human rights advocate of El Salvador]. Boston, MA: South End Press.

Washington Post Staff. 2015. "Full Text: Donald Trump Announces a Presidential Bid." *Washington Post,* June 16, 2015. https://www.washingtonpost.com/news/post-politics/wp/2015/06/16/full-text-donald-trump-announces-a-presidential-bid/.

Yarris, Kristin. 2022. "Narrative Testimony and Political Potentiality: Surviving Family Separation, Advocating for Migrants' Rights and Well-Being." In *Migration and Health: Challenging the Borders of Belonging, Care, and Policy,* edited by Nadia El-Shaaarawi and Stéphanie Larchaché, 173–190. New York: Berghahn Books.

CHAPTER 8

Convivencia

Storytelling as Accompaniment, Activism, and Care

ERIKA VARGAS REYES, LUPE LÓPEZ, AND WHITNEY L. DUNCAN

Convivencia

I (WLD) have been thinking about accompaniment for a long time. Or, rather, I have been thinking about *convivencia* for a long time. As I wrote in my 2018 book on mental health in Mexico, "the Spanish word *convivir* has multiple meanings: to live in the company of others, to get along with others, to coexist with others, to visit with and interact with others. I view anthropological research and writing as a long process of being-with, or convivencia" (Duncan 2018, xiii). But even as I wrote those words, I felt troubled by the ways my ethnographic work was haunted by the inequalities, extractive tendencies, and "basic coloniality" that shape the anthropological project (Bejarano et al. 2019, 36). I have always wanted to "write with," not "write for" (Martínez Luna 2010, 19); I have always wanted my work to center care, co-presence, and actions of pragmatic solidarity (Farmer 1999). But while I was committed to these ideals, I was not always sure how to actualize them.

This changed around the time I started working with the Denver-based *Ni1Más Deportación* (Not1More Deportation) group in the aftermath of the 2016 election. *Ni1Más*, a sub-group of American Friends Service Committee, is a support and advocacy group for individuals and families in deportation proceedings. The group is composed of directly impacted immigrant members who provide accompaniment and mutual support, engage in advocacy and trainings, and—crucially—who seek to transform policy both locally and federally. As I learned more about the accompaniment model and began accompanying Ni1Más members to ICE check-ins, in their court proceedings, to doctors' visits, as they navigated services and policies, and in direct actions like marches, demonstrations, fasts, and vigils, my whole orientation toward ethnographic work shifted.[1] This was convivencia, but with teeth—a way of being-with that decentered my own role as ethnographer and prioritized relationality, collaborative action, mutual care, and structural change. This was accompaniment.

But why stories? Ni1Más members like my coauthors share powerful personal stories in many contexts: in research interviews, at immigrant-rights rallies, at press conferences, in legislative meetings, and in court proceedings. In these contexts, they insist upon their own rights and humanity, both of which are constantly called into question by the U.S. immigration system that seeks to exclude them. Sometimes in those stories "the experience of suffering is appropriated or alienated from the subject and transformed" into what Erica Caple James calls "trauma portfolios," forms of currency in immigration proceedings and humanitarian markets—and, I would add, in scholarly knowledge production—symbolic of one's perceived deservingness and worth (James 2004, 131). What would happen if we worked together to create a new narrative space anchored in the insistence that participants are always already deserving and that their stories are worth telling in and of themselves? Convivencia was born out of this question.

Of course, over the years that we've worked together, the branches of friendship, activism, family, and ethnography have become increasingly intertwined. As Lopez, Kline, LeBrón, and Novak discuss in their contribution to this volume, accompaniment as an approach unapologetically embraces these layered relations, and the collaborative storytelling process we use in Convivencia both reflects and deepens them. Rooted in relation, affect, and action, Convivencia blends the personal and political to challenge dominant portrayals of undocumented immigrants and to create spaces of mutual care and healing.

The fact that we are friends, *activistas*, and fellow mothers who nonetheless occupy very different positionalities yields certain forms of re-

1. See Duncan 2018 for additional discussion of accompaniment in the group.

flection and conversation that I hope come across in the project. My privilege facilitates my ability to provide accompaniment in Convivencia and other contexts: I have relative freedom over my time, I am not living precariously or worried about my immigration status, and I do not experience discrimination due to my skin color or language. I use this privilege—as well as my training as an ethnographer, my commitment to social justice, and my love and admiration for these friends—to help make Convivencia possible, to hold space for the sharing, to perform some of the nitty gritty work in the background so that my *colaboradoras* can focus on their stories and on the being-with—the convivencia—when we are engaged in project work.[2]

In many ways, like the project Hansen and Robles Robles describe in the preceding chapter, Convivencia is inspired by Latin American traditions of *testimonio*, "crucial means of bearing witness and inscribing into history those lived realities that would otherwise succumb to the alchemy of erasure" (Latina Feminist Group 2001, 2). We have tended to use the word "*historias*" instead, which feels more expansive than testimonios, but which leaves open the possibility of story as political action. Unlike the more traditional testimonio, "a form of expression that comes out of intense repression or struggle, where a person bearing witness tells the story to someone else, who then transcribes, edits, translates, and publishes the text elsewhere" (Latina Feminist Group 2001, 13), Convivencia is an ongoing, long-term, dialogic process of accompaniment. But if testimonios are forms of political resistance, acts of coalition-, consciousness-, and community-building, and if they are also forms of

2. The broader project includes a growing number of additional women; EV and LL are two of the initial women who helped conceive of the project idea and who I first sat down with for unstructured storytelling sessions. We decided to record these sessions and to let them flow freely, without predetermined goals or themes. I took field notes during the sessions, paid for the recordings to be transcribed, and highlighted themes within them that seemed particularly salient. I then shared back the transcripts for EV and LL to read, comment on, and edit, and we had additional exchanges about how to structure each historia and which to include for this chapter. Because EV and LL primarily speak Spanish, we wanted the whole chapter to appear in English and Spanish; however, we were limited by space constraints. Therefore, we decided to include Spanish translations of all direct quotations and story excerpts, and we plan to publish the full Spanish translation on an associated website.

personal and collective healing and reclaiming, we consider Convivencia, too, as a practice of testimonio.[3]

Convivencia lends itself to first-person stories and reflections; second-person letters (see Duncan 2022); snippets from WhatsApp texts and voice recordings; personal documents, scraps, and archives (what the Latina Feminist Group calls *papelitos guardados*); and excerpts from fieldnotes, transcripts, and phone calls. We integrate elements of collaborative ethnography, oral history, personal narrative, and creative writing, as well. In the future, we hope to include multimedia components and to have in-person group convenings. As one would expect, the project builds momentum and then sputters as each of us confronts the mundane and extraordinary challenges of living, working, parenting, and engaging in activism and accompaniment. Yes, the project would proceed more quickly with an abundance of long, languorous afternoons filled with delicious food and sharing. We have no funding, we have small children and jobs, we have little time, and yet we have much desire. So, the work continues at its pace as its own form of care and commitment. We hope the project reflects the ways our being-together unfolds during this particular political and historical moment.

Storytelling as Accompaniment

> *Even in my darkest recollection, there was someone singing my life back to me.*
>
> —NEKO CASE, *GUIDED BY WIRE*

Queridas Colaboradoras, Cuentistas, Narradoras, Testimoniadoras: This has been one of my (WLD's) favorite songs for nearly twenty years now. It popped into my head as I sat down to begin writing this piece, and it kept returning as I sat down again and again to read and listen to your stories and all the fragments and artifacts of research and accompaniment we have generated over the years. I am moved by the idea of how others can sing our lives back to us, accompany us, conjure us back to ourselves in a full-throated voice.

3. See Angueira 1988; Anzaldúa 1989; Espino et al. 2012; Freire 1973; Hansen and Robles Robles 2021; Huber 2009; Blackmer Reyes and Rodriquez 2012; Latina Feminist Group 2001; Urrieta and Villenas 2013.

This storytelling project is a space for you to sing yourselves back to yourselves, with supportive accompaniment. To remember, to reclaim, and to revivify. There is a healing in the telling, the crafting, the sharing—"stories are medicine," the psychoanalyst Clarissa Pinkola Estés writes (1995, 15)—and I don't need to cite theory for you to know that. Here, stories are a form of care, a form of pleasure. We talk a lot about *la lucha*—and about how, to keep ourselves engaged in la lucha, we must also laugh, linger in the flavor of *mango con chamoy* on the tongue, sense sides of ourselves that some would deny us.

As I help facilitate your tellings, I read adrienne maree brown's work on pleasure activism: "The work we do to reclaim our whole, happy, and satisfiable selves from the impacts, delusions, and limitations of oppression and/or supremacy" (brown 2019, 16), and sigh, *yes*. Because what is possible when we make space together to gather our bones under a late-summer sun?

You knew the answer the instant we started conceiving of this project: I could see it in the way you smiled and gently closed your eyes, saying, *sí, me gustaría*, or in the way your voice softened over the phone. In your expressions: pleasure, and with pleasure, a kind of freedom, and with freedom, a renewed drive toward justice. adrienne maree brown asks, "What would happen if we aligned with a pleasure politic, especially as people who are surviving long-term oppressive conditions?" I hope for Convivencia to pose an answer to that question.

These are your stories on the page; your music, your knowing, your archives, your poetry, your pleasure. These are not your case files. These are a different form of documentation. Of course, you are storytellers in many contexts; sometimes by choice and often by necessity. You are storytelling to survive, singing a clear path ahead for yourselves, for your families.

Those stories have a *fin*, a goal; they are in service *of*. You must tell them the way you do because of the perverted logics inherent to systems that demand them. Those stories, collected in manifold documents—affidavits, declarations, applications—that are nevertheless not the *right* documents, center trauma, violence, exclusion.

But what of the stories that come out the side of the mouth when the front is storytelling to *sobrevivir*? What currency are the sitting-at-the-park-eating-melon stories, the stories that rise in the steam of the *caldo* you're stirring? What of the stories you retell as you feed your chickens, that you recall singing hymns at the church that saved you? The stories that bring with them the feel of your mother's hand on the small of your back, the smell of her famous *pollo con tajadas,* the breath of wind through trees in a place you felt safe, the sound of each of your children's first cries?

Here, there is no case to win, no law to pass, no program to qualify for, no proof to gather. No sound bite for reporters, no theories to illustrate with you as exemplar, no wounds to reopen as evidence of. Not for now, at least. In Convivencia, we create a space of solidarity, connection, and co-presence. Your stories here do not shy from pain, but the pain is the flip side of the pleasure; the pain is not the proof.

This, too, is a political act; a creative act of refusal, a caring for and a being-with through story. It is an insistence on the right to be in your bodies, in your homes, in your families. On the right to conjure through poetry, resist through testimonio, rest in friendship. Insistence, too, on the right to rights you've been arbitrarily denied and I've been arbitrarily afforded: the right to take deep, full breaths in whichever country you choose; visit your birthlands; live free of violence and state terror; have access to policies and programs that include you; work; tend your gardens; and stir your pots without fear of who might knock on your door to take it all away, or take you away from all of it.

Here's our vision, here's our aspiration. Here, you shape stories and testimonios in your own voices. Here you are in your fullness, strength, vulnerability, rage, faith, tears, and raucous laughter. Here, together, we sing ourselves back to ourselves.

What This Wind Is Doing

It is late October, and the wind is blowing all the yellow leaves off the trees; fall carnage. Trees thinning themselves toward winter. The sky is scrubbed clean, brilliant blue, as though even the clouds can't hang on. I (WLD) arrive at E's door with two coffees in hand, a few clementines tucked in my bag. E's seventeen-year-old daughter, K, is home from school; she is hanging Halloween decorations in the dining room when I enter. K smiles shyly and retreats into her bedroom. E is on the phone with a family member in Mexico. She takes the coffee and the small container of sugar, mouths *gracias,* and sets them on the table.

The house is cold. We cover ourselves in blankets as we sit on the couch. I am not entirely sure what to expect: we haven't made a plan, per se. We have discussed the idea for Convivencia to be a space for E and others to reflect, remember, gather up threads and weave something they can hold in their hands, share with their children. My role is to listen, accompany, doula the delivery.

When we met several years before, E's youngest daughter, M, was still a babe-in-arms, like my youngest. E's husband was detained at GEO, the Immigration and Customs Enforcement (ICE) processing and detention center in Aurora, Colorado. What I remember from that meeting was the look that came over E's face, the way her eyes sparkled when she started to share, as though she were delivering a spoken-word poem, as though she were in the pulpit.

Seated in E's living room, sometimes I wonder if E remembers I am there; it's as though she's in a kind of rapture at times, the pleasure of telling—even the painful parts. Once or twice, I remind E of the coffee, lukewarm by now, still sitting on the table behind us. *"Al rato" (in a bit),* she says, gesturing lightly, continuing her story.

At its center, the roiling heart of it, are E's parents; her story of departure, crossing, and arrival; and the joys, pleasures, and pains of mothering. There is also poetry, and the way E's words and body make space for memory, hope, and unshakeable determination. The transcript from that day is forty-five pages, single-spaced—I read it closely as I re-listen to her voice telling it. I realize it is a story told in ten parts, punctuated by a dream interlude. I make headings for ease of reading, print it out, drop it off at E's house along with some clothes my daughters have outgrown that I think M would like.

I. *Niñez* / Childhood
II. *El Camino y los Primeros Tenis* / The Journey and the First Sneakers
III. *La Llegada* / Arrival
IV. *La Vida de una Mama* / A Mother's Life
V. *Sueño: Cayendo del Suelo* / Dream: Falling from the Sky
VI. *Matrimonio, Maternidad y las Héridas de Infancia* / Marriage, Motherhood, and Childhood Wounds
VII. *La Historia de Separarme de mi Primer Pareja* / Separating from my First Partner

VIII. *Matrimonio Actual* / Current Marriage
IX. *La Activista: Enfrentando la Injusticia* / The Activist: Confronting Injustice
X. *Esperanzas* / Hopes

Months pass. Life intervenes. Also, this is difficult work, and E takes on a job as a cleaner and so cannot meet during the day. We message, we talk on the phone, we attend Ni1Más meetings, we organize assistance for another friend and Ni1Más member. E texts me daily when I am sick with COVID-19; it's one of the only things that makes me smile from the depths of my exhaustion.

no te angusties porque le das fuerza al covid	don't worry because it strengthens covid
Yo se que es dificil pero piensa positivo🙏🙏	I know it's hard but think positive🙏🙏
Recuerda eres una mujer joven fuerte y sobretodo Fuerte ante las adversidades de la vida 💪💪🌹🌹🌹🌹🌹🌹💐💐💐💐💐💐💐💐💐💐	Remember you're a strong young woman and above all Strong in the face of life's adversities 💪💪🌹🌹🌹🌹🌹🌹💐💐💐💐💐💐💐💐💐💐

As I am waiting for the stars to align so we can meet again and talk about her historia—what it is like to read her own words, what elements she wants to highlight, develop, remove—I find myself thinking about how E uses metaphor. When her stories are really cooking, she starts to speak in poetry. I extract an example from the final section, *Esperanzas* (Hopes). It's page 32 of the transcript, part of her response to my question of how adjusting her status—having residency or citizenship, having papers—would change her life.

Immediately E responds:

pues eso cambiaría mucho, principalmente porque podría visitar a mis papás, podría visitar a mi mamá . . . Sería como descansar, como tener paz, tener tranquilidad, tener más seguridad. Siento que nos están haciendo valer como seres humanos, no por el color, sino por lo que valemos por personas. Y creo que también nuestros hijos vivirían más tranquilos.

that would change so much, mainly because I could visit my parents, I could visit my mother . . . It would be like resting, like having peace, having tranquility, having more security. It would show that we count as human beings, not because of our color, but because of what we are worth as people. And I think our children would also live more peacefully.

E then discusses how her children remain traumatized by her husband's detention, and how her daughter K recently asked her how you get "papers" and what they are for. E explained to K that when someone is born in the United States, they automatically get a social security number. "Ese seguro social es tu permiso para trabajar. Y le digo, pero cuando nosotros llegamos y no tenemos nada." *(That social security number is your permission to work. And I tell her, but when we get here we have nothing like that.)*

Then E pauses for a moment, looking into the distance. She says:

siento	I feel
como si fuéramos hojas	as if we were leaves
así como ahorita—	just like right now—
que está haciendo este viento.	what is this wind doing.
Que andamos, siento que hasta	we walk, I feel that even
andamos hasta	we walk
volando en el aire	flying in the air
no tenemos algo fijo	nothing is secure for us
algún rumbo como que ahorita	no fixed course so now
que somos estas hojas.	we are these leaves.
Ahorita no hace aire,	Right now without wind
estamos acá.	we're here.

Hasta el aire nos va a ir a llevar
hasta por allá lejos

Then the wind will take us
all the way over there

Igual así nosotros.

Same with us.

Ahorita estamos acá.

Right now we are here.

Si el día de mañana nos topamos
con migración—
dónde quedó lo que fuimos?
Dónde quedó lo que tuvimos,
dónde quedó
a dónde estábamos?

If tomorrow we run into
immigration—
where was what we were?
Where was what we had?
where was it
where were we?

Es como si no estuvimos,
como no existes.
me entiendes?
Automáticamente no existimos.

It is as if we're nothing
like you don't exist
do you understand me?
We do not automatically exist.

Estamos, pero no estamos.
Aquí estamos, pero no nos ven!

We are, but we are not.
Here we are, but you don't see us!

Aquí estoy, pero no soy.

Here I am, but I am not.

* * *

I title the poem "Hojas," por E. Vargas, and text it to her.

W: mire, escribiste un poema.
¿Qué piensas?

W: look, you wrote a poem.
What do you think?

E: Dejame checar
Y te aviso

E: let me check
and I'll let you know

W: Lo extraje de tu transcripción.
Es hermoso 🍃🍂

W: I took it from your transcript.
It's beautiful 🍃🍂

E: 😍

E: 😍

* * *

When I step away from it, though, I begin to worry that I am romanticizing. If E had wanted to write a poem, she would have written one. And "extracting" a poem, polishing words so they gleam—well, the word "extract" says enough.[4] When I sit down with "Hojas" again, though, I recall that E's metaphors don't sugarcoat. When E says she feels like she and other undocumented folks are wind-blown leaves, she is referring to her lack of control over her own story; she is referring to her own possible erasure. And, by telling her stories, by speaking her poems, using imagery as playful and pleasurable as airborne leaves in autumn, she is reclaiming.

Each summer, I wonder how the leaves that fell the autumn before managed to disappear so quickly, frozen beneath snow, dissolved into spring's rot. "*Aqui estoy, pero no soy*," E says. Here, in these pages, you are.

Motherfruit: Así Como Ella / Just Like Her

L and I do her first Convivencia sessions via Zoom—her car broke down, and we live over an hour from each other—but I have seen L share stories in many different contexts over the more than five years I have known her. At my first Ni1Más meeting, I heard the story of how her immigration case—which she has been fighting for over a decade—began. I have heard other parts at rallies and protests, vigils outside GEO, press conferences, at her final court hearing. I have watched U.S. senators choke up as they listen to her; I have read some of her stories in the news.

Often when I see L on Zoom meetings, she is stirring pots or pressing tortillas in the kitchen as she calls after her five children. On this summer day, she appears in a room painted a cheerful poppy-red. L's yellow

4. Also, I can't get Karla Cornejo Villavicencio's voice out of my head—in particular, the way she writes about how "migrants are celebrated through art that strikes me as deeply annoying, mostly the word 'migrant' reconfigured as butterflies. I fucking hate thinking of migrants as butterflies" (2020, 12). Cornejo Villavicencio critiques the seemingly inevitable binaries through which media—and political and often academic discourse—represent migrants: as demons or angels, criminals or victims, undeserving drains on the system or "essential workers" propping up the economy. Rarely do they appear in narratives as complex, beautifully imperfect humans, like all humans are.

sleeveless top contrasts beautifully with the walls and makes me think of sunflower fields. She wears a gold necklace that sways as she speaks; sometimes she slides the charm back and forth on its chain.

* * *

L's stories are best paired with some of her favorite things: mole rojo con arroz rojo; "tortillas hechas a mano calientitas"; pepino, melón, *cushin* fruit; un vasito de arroz con leche *(hot handmade tortillas, cucumber, melon, cushin fruit, a cup of rice pudding).* Bury your feet in the earth by a river as you read, as L likes to do as she recalls her favorite, most dulce *memorias* of childhood.

Her chickens cluck in the background as she begins:

> Me emociona mucho porque fue una parte dura, pero también ahorita de mamá, he reflexionado y realmente hay muchas cosas muy bonitas en esa parte.
>
> Mi mamá fue una madre muy buena, de verdad que yo le estoy tan agradecida a Dios porque me haya dado una mamá así. Siempre fue responsable con nosotros, siempre estuvo en las reuniones en la escuela, nunca nos dejó y es por eso que yo como madre ahora yo lo vivo, yo digo, "Yo quiero ser así como ella."
>
> . . . Pues nosotros en nuestra familia no tuvimos dinero. Tuvimos problemas económicos, pero fue muy lindo porque nos dábamos mucho amor.
>
> Mi madre le gustaba mucho vender frutas allá en Chiapas, es un lugar tan bonito que se da todo tipo de frutas. Yo recuerdo muy bien los melones, sandías, pepinos, hay otras frutas que le dicen cushin, pero es como paternas, unas largas, que tienen como que fueran algodones, pero están bien ricos.
>
> Mi mamá era vendedora de toda clase de frutas, de esta manera nos ayudábamos económicamente porque ella le gustaba ir a un mercado, está en Ciudad Hidalgo, Chiapas. Es un mercado bien lindo porque hay todo tipo de cosas, de frutas, de colores, de sabores. Yo recuerdo que me iba siempre a esa plaza porque, como te digo, nunca mi mamá nos dejaba solos, ella estaba con su venta ahí, podíamos compartir con otras personas que también estaban vendiendo en ese mercado.

Algo que me recuerda mucho es que nos desayunábamos un pan y un vasito de arroz con leche. Mi mamá ahí en el mercado vendía, mi mamá nos compraba un pan y un vasito de arroz con leche. Nosotros lo disfrutábamos tanto.

I get emotional because it's a difficult story, but I have reflected a lot about my mother and there are really many very beautiful things there.

My mom was a very good mother. I'm so grateful to God for giving me a mom like that. She was always responsible with us, she was always at school meetings, she never left us. That's why now, as a mother, I live it and I say, "I want to be just like her."

. . . Well, in our family we had no money. We had financial problems, but it was still beautiful because we gave each other a lot of love.

My mother really liked to sell fruit in Chiapas—it is such a beautiful place that produces all kinds of fruit. I distinctly remember the melons, watermelons, cucumbers . . . There are other fruits that are called cushin—they're like paternas, long and like cotton, but they are very tasty.

My mother sold all kinds of fruits—this is how we helped financially, because she liked to go to a market in Ciudad Hidalgo, Chiapas. It is a very nice market since there are all kinds of things: fruits, colors, flavors. I remember that I always went to the plaza because, as I told you, my mom never left us alone, she was selling her fruit and we could share with other people in the market.

Something I often remember is that we used to have bread and a glass of rice pudding for breakfast. My mother there in the market, bringing us bread and a glass of rice pudding. We enjoyed it so much.

* * *

L is six years old, perched with her brothers at the entrance of a beautiful church, waiting for their mother to finish selling at the market. L is "hablando con Dios y pidiéndole para que mi mamá pudiera terminar su venta del día, todas las cosas que llevaba. Estaba yo bien contenta hablando con Dios y te digo que siempre me daba una paz espiritual" *(talking to God and asking him for my mom to finish her sales for the day, to sell everything she brought. I was very happy talking with God and I tell you that it always gave me spiritual peace).*

Soon, a kindly tourist approaches L and asks if she can photograph L and her brothers. She says yes, and, after taking the photograph the woman asks, "¿Qué andan haciendo tan solitos?" *(What are you doing here so alone?)*

L responds, "No, no estamos solitos. Aquí a un ladito está mi mamá, ella está ahí vendiendo en el mercado, pero no estamos solos" *(No, we're not alone. My mother is just over there, selling at the market, but we're not alone).*

The woman tells L that she would love to help them, to give them some money. I wonder where the photograph is now, the one of L and her brothers, barefoot at the church entrance. L recalls the "*rollito de dinero*" (little roll of cash) that the woman handed her, but not how much it was—L could not yet count. She does remember, though, how happy her mother was when L handed it to her; it was enough to put shoes on their feet and buy food for a week.

From then on, L always wanted to help her mother, to see that smile.

First, at eight years old, L worked at Señora Nati's carnicería *(butcher)* doing *mandados* (errands), helping customers with their heavy bags of food. When she grew into a señorita, L labored in the *bananeros,* the *empacadoras (banana fields and packing plants)* in Chiapas and then in Guatemala. There, she encountered too many *sinvergüenzas (shameless scoundrels)* to count. Fortunately, L said, "mi mamá me enseñó que yo me tenía que defender" *(my mother taught me that I had to defend myself),* but soon, things got so bad that L had to leave.

El Hubiera Ya No Existe / What Could Have Been Doesn't Exist Now

L never meant to stay in the United States—she wanted to be by her mother's side always. To see her mother's smile, to taste the fruit her mother sold. The idea was to work *en el norte* for a few years, save up enough to help her mother build a kitchen. Maybe, L thought, she could even start a business back home.

> Yo decía, "Con tres años me alcanza para poder yo ayudar a mi madre a hacer una concina." A tener un dinerito, una tienda, porque siempre fue

> mi sueño tener una tiendita. Una tienda a la orilla de la calle, ahí donde yo podía vender raspados, donde yo podía vender sodas, cositas como comida. Yo deseaba esto. Yo decía, "Así no voy a tener la necesidad de andar trabajando en lugares donde hay personas malas. Teniendo mi propio negocito yo solita, voy a poder salir adelante y ayudar a mi familia."

> I used to say, "Three years is enough for me to help my mother build a kitchen." To have some money, a store—because it was always my dream to have a little store. A store on the side of the street where I could sell shaved ice, where I could sell sodas, snacks. I wanted this. I said, "This way I won't have to work in places where there are bad people. Having my own little business by myself, I will be able to get ahead and help my family."

But the moment L arrived at the airport in Chiapas, she regretted her decision.

> Yo sentía un dolor grandísimo, un nudo aquí en la garganta, un dolor en el pecho que no podía respirar bien, que me sentía mal, pero tampoco quería llorar, porque no quería demostrarle a mi mamá que estaba arrepentida o lo que no quería es que me viera llorando porque yo sé que también ella iba a llorar. Me hice la fuerte y creo que cometí un error ahí.

> I felt such grief, a lump here in my throat, a pain in my chest so I couldn't breathe well. I felt bad, but I didn't want to cry either, because I didn't want to show my mom that I regretted my decision. I didn't want her to see me crying because I knew that she was going to cry too. I pretended to be strong and I think I made a mistake there.

L hugged her mother goodbye and boarded the airplane. She said that, when it took off,

> yo recuerdo muy bien, yo lo vi todo tan chiquito. Fue mi primera vez que yo subí en un avión. Lo miré tan pequeñito, tan pequeñito. Parte de mi corazón sentía que se me salía en ese momento. Estaba yo llorando y pensando en mi mamá, en mis hermanitos. Ya no los iba a poder ver por un gran tiempo.

> I remember it very well, everything looked so small. It was my first time on a plane. Everything looked so tiny, so tiny. Part of my heart felt like it left me at that moment. I was crying and thinking about my mom, about my little brothers. I was not going to be able to see them for a long time.

But it was more than a "gran tiempo"; L would never see her mother again. She became ill and died four months after L arrived in the United States.

> Yo a veces me pongo a pensar, "¿Y si no me hubiera venido? ¿Y si me hubiera quedado con mi mamá?" Pero el hubiera ya no existe.

> I sometimes start to think, "What if I hadn't come? What if I had stayed with my mother?" But what could have been doesn't exist now.

* * *

Soon, L must go collect her daughter from summer camp. She is still crying, and I thank her, tell her how *conmovida* I am.

"*Gracias a ti por escucharme*," L responds.

> Porque esto me sirve como una terapia, platicar, sacar las cosas. Te duele, pero al mismo tiempo también puedes desahogarte y sacar lo que uno está pasando, ¿no?

> Thank you for listening to me. Because is like therapy for me, to talk, to get things out. It hurts, but at the same time you can also unburden yourself and get out what you're going through, right?

We resolve to pick up the story another day soon, maybe in person. The next part, L says, "es un poquito dolorosa, pero más buena que mala." A little bit painful, but more good than bad.

> Porque lo más bonito que yo tengo y que me da fuerza en este momento, y que me siento la mujer más, se podría decir, que estuviera rica, millonaria, son mis hijos. Ellos me han dado tanta alegría. Es algo tan bonito.

Because the most beautiful thing that I have and that gives me strength at this moment—and that I feel like the most woman, one could say, that I was rich, a millionaire—are my children. They have given me so much joy. It's such a beautiful thing.

She laughs, looking up again, the pleasure plain on her face.

References

Angueira, Katherine. 1988. "To Make the Personal Political: The Use of Testimony as a Consciousness Raising Tool against Sexual Aggression in Puerto Rico." *Oral History Review* 16 (2): 65–93.

Anzaldúa, Gloria. 1989. *Borderlands/La Frontera: The New Mestiza*. 2nd ed. San Francisco, CA: Aunt Lute Books.

Bejarano, Carolina Alonso, Lucia López Juárez, Mirian Mijangos García, and Daniel Goldstein. 2019. *Decolonizing Ethnography: Undocumented Immigrants and New Directions in Social Science*. Durham, NC: Duke University Press.

Blackmer Reyes, Kathryn, and Julia E. Curry Rodríguez. 2012. "Testimonio: Origins, Terms, and Resources." *Equity and Excellence in Education* 45 (3): 525–538.

brown, adrienne maree, ed. 2019. *Pleasure Activism: The Politics of Feeling Good*. Chico, CA: AK Press.

Duncan, Whitney L. 2018. "*Acompañamiento/Accompaniment.*" Society for Cultural Anthropology. https://culanth.org/fieldsights/1289-acompanamiento-accompaniment.

Duncan, Whitney L. 2022. "Dear D." *American Anthropologist*. June 2022. https://www.americananthropologist.org/online-content/dear-d.

Espino, Michelle M., Irene I. Vega, Laura I. Rendón, Jessica J. Ranero, and Marcela M. Muñiz. 2012. "The Process of Reflexión in Bridging Testimonios across Lived Experience: Michelle M. Espino Irene I." *Equity and Excellence in Education* 45 (3): 444–459.

Estés, Clarissa Pinkola. 1995. *Women Who Run with the Wolves: Myths and Stories of the Wild Woman Archetype*. New York: Ballantine Books.

Farmer, Paul. 1999. "Pathologies of Power: Rethinking Health and Human Rights." *American Journal of Public Health* 89 (10): 1486–1496.

Freire, Paolo. 1973. *Pedagogy of the Oppressed*. New York: Seabury.

Hansen, Tobin, and María Engracia Robles Robles. 2021. *Voices of the Border: Testimonios of Migration, Deportation, and Asylum*. Washington, D.C.: Georgetown University Press.

Huber, Lindsay Pérez. 2009. "Disrupting Apartheid of Knowledge: Testimonio as Methodology in Latina/o Critical Race Research in Education." *International Journal of Qualitative Studies in Education* 22 (6): 639–654.

James, Erica Caple. 2004. "The Political Economy of 'Trauma' in Haiti in the Democratic Era of Insecurity." *Culture, Medicine and Psychiatry* 28 (2): 127–149.
Latina Feminist Group. 2001. "Introduction: *Papelitos Guardados: Theorizing* Latinidades Through *Testimonio*." In *Telling to Live: Latina Feminist Testimonios*, edited by Luz del Alba Acevedo, 1–24. Durham, NC: Duke University Press.
Martínez Luna, Jaime. 2010. *Eso que llaman comunalidad*. Oaxaca, México: Culturas Populares, CONACULRA/Secretaría de Cultura, Gobierno de Oaxaca/Fundación Alfredo Harp Helú.
Urrieta, L. Jr., and Villenas, S. A. 2013. "The Legacy of Derrick Bell and Latino/a Education: A Critical Race Testimonio." *Race Ethnicity and Education* 16 (4): 514–535.
Villavicencio, Karla Cornejo. 2020. *The Undocumented Americans*. New York: One World.

PART IV

Concluding Reflections: Accompaniment and Caring Anthropology

CHAPTER 9

Accompaniment as Moral and Political Practices

Possibilities and Challenges

JOSIAH HEYMAN

Vibrant transnational migration coexists with coercive repression. This occurs in a contradictory situation where labor demand intersects with xenophobic reaction against the movement of people toward that demand, with the addition of people fleeing violence and persecution (Heyman 2012). An important example of this is the short-circuiting of asylum by the wealthy countries of the world (FitzGerald 2019), which we can capture in the term "global apartheid" (Besteman 2020).

People thus face situations where movement is reasonable and even necessary. Yet they also face situations where movement is punished with death, imprisonment (detention), forcible expulsion, and extended legal persecution (see Gomberg-Muñoz 2017 for a concise summary of these themes in U.S. immigration policy). The settings of these issues fall roughly into three parts: the places from which people start to move, which, after decades of migration are intimately linked to destinations; the passages up to and through heavily policed borders; and while living inside places of arrival, sometimes securely but often under threat, both physical and legal.

An important context for many of the chapters here, though not all, is ambiguous life inside receiving countries (see Horton 2020), in which people face possible arrest and deportation, ripping them from their families, communities, and jobs. They do not just occupy a simple legal status (even legal migrants and in some cases citizens) but rather multiple statuses and positions that to varied extents allow them to develop webs of activities and social relations but at the same time entail threatened or actual tears in the fabric of such everyday life. Accompaniment, it seems to me, is particularly drawn toward these sorts of present but potentially disappeared circumstances, because it is a method of knowing, connecting, and morally and politically affirming humanity and mutuality in contexts where such connections fully exist but may be suddenly destroyed.

This current moment of movement-with-exclusion is not just a circumstance we observe and analyze from outside; it is a setting for intense political-ethical struggle. Accompaniment should be understood in this context. The chapters here acknowledge openly and honestly their "sidedness," their affiliation with moral and political positions in the current struggle. That is a crucial character of accompaniment. As compellingly illustrated in the chapter by Vargas et al., we connect with particular people in specific circumstances and emotionally loaded ways, not in an arm's length, often illusorily objectivist way. Human connection is fundamental to ethics, and politics are the way we act ethically. Our topics, connections, and knowledge products have value implications that are inherent and cannot be avoided by hiding behind a false idea of what science is. Science, especially social science, is a kind of action in the world, as much as professional scholarship hides and denies it, and action among fellow people invariably brings complex ethical choices. Accompaniment's foundational strength is that it acknowledges and builds on this. Following that realization, the choices of ethics and politics—who to accompany and why—require and deserve thoughtful reflection and articulate discussion, as demonstrated in this book.

The chapters here are rich with accounts of accompaniment in action, broaching questions that need to be asked and lessons that can be usefully learned. In previous work documenting and analyzing experiences as a social scientist-activist, I have argued that we should provide deep, critical ethnography of what actually occurs in radical practices to go along with more abstracted and idealized advocacy for them (Heyman 2011, 2015). Here, we can draw from the richness of the book to identify possibilities, alternative approaches, and challenges in the radical moral-political practice of accompaniment.

Many times in these chapters, we see change over time in the situation, relationship, and thus the kind of accompaniment. Nuñez-Janes and Heiman describe the evolution of a short-term, problem-solving university-community partnership, a university student-staffed helpline for K–12 student questions about assignments during a period when they had been sent home because of COVID-19, into an enduring societal alliance transcending its ostensible practical purpose, which had ended as pupils returned to school. It had gone from being beneficent help to true accompaniment. Getrich et al. trace a change from a university-community consultative board into an enduring small group, a friendship network of non-migrants and migrants of diverse legal statuses. They defied the pandemic and spatial fragmentation though regular online get-togethers. The authors also narrate the eventual breakup of this group as, inevitably, people move on in their lives. They term the outcome of this development from single-purpose organization to tight social group a "multivalent mode of practice," finely capturing a potential, often realized, in accompaniment. Indeed, the evolution from narrow pragmatic purpose to emotional bonding and rich social ties cuts across all the chapters of the book. Accompaniment is not just a single fixed act but also a process of relating.

The book narrates a range of kinds of action within or connected to accompaniment. The power setting, specific lines of struggle, and webs of relationships in that context need to be considered carefully in order to discern what sort of action, accompaniment of various kinds and other sorts of tactics, is particularly needed. For example, fully revealed and expressed shared humanity—the essence of accompaniment—is paramount in the struggle against xenophobic and racist othering, as richly communicated in the chapters by Lopez et al. and Vargas et al. At the same time, more distanced scientific methods can provide important results and garner recognition (e.g., Lopez et al. 2021, 2022). It will be productive to have a wide, tolerant, and flexible attitude to tactics in the struggle: What do we need to defeat racism, exploitation, and xenophobia? How does accompaniment add to already-existing formal methods to bring a stronger whole in the field of struggle?

Likewise, accompaniment is itself diverse and complex. The chapter by Escalante Villagrán et al. points out how accompaniment may not be simply becoming equal (something that probably is never fully possible). In that case, Heidbrink's resources in the United States and her educated skill set to organize flows of support worked in a division of labor with collective organizers in Guatemala confronting bias and repression during COVID-19. Accompaniment has an ethos of equality and mutuality, but in making effective struggle, difference was actually a crucial resource. Likewise, Hansen and Robles Robles challenge us to stretch our idea of what accompaniment is. They explore how *testimonios* that they collected and published might offer the opportunity for readers to vicariously accompany migrants. They are suitably cautious about claiming this as full accompaniment in the enduring and personal sense seen in other case studies, but they make a valuable point: Accompaniment in person is limited in the number of people who can be involved. Connecting on a personal level, albeit imaginative, through testimonios enables a wider audience to have a relationship of sorts with migrants. This in turn can help the pro-migrant struggle.

Finally, in the book's wide-ranging observations of accompaniment, we encounter many interpersonal and collective political-ethical choices. These moral choices are not simple; that is an important finding of carefully observing and reporting on the actual practice of accompaniment. A telling example is Yarris's chapter that narrates the dilemmas of deservingness judgments. They emerge in a situation of greater need for bonds for release from detention than can be accommodated by a limited bond fund. The lesson likely goes beyond this case; our capacity (time, energy, material goods, and emotional reservoirs) will almost always be far less than the universe of possibilities.

Likewise, in the world of immigration, it bears observing that moral choices of working with or for particular people are not simple. Some migrants have troubling backgrounds (Campbell, Slack, and Diedrich 2017). Their legal defense advocacy is important; standing up for asylum and protection from torture are principles that merit action, even for problematic people. There are questions we always should ask. Who do we accompany? And what values do we choose by accompanying that person or those people? Often, migration in the face of global apartheid renders such compelling stories that the rationales for our moral choices almost go unstated. Migration today faces repressive, inhumane, and racist responses. The suffering entailed is emotionally compelling—with good reason. But that may render our sense of what is implied in the process of personal and moral affiliation too simple for what actually is and should be involved in making choices of relationship and alignment.

The moral and political terrain of the many various struggles where we accompany people is surely varied and complex. The answer is not to abandon relationship-making but to engage in thoughtful and thorough dialogue about our moral navigation when we do it. These complex questions of tactics and relationships need to be in some reasonable equilibrium, keeping in mind that the greater goal is transforming the current world of terror and exclusion.

Accompaniment, in the end, offers two important lessons for activist anthropology. One is opening up our sources of actionable knowledge to include the knowledge brought by our partners in political struggle. This is not to dismiss the value of strong, critical observation and analysis, done by professional social scientists. It is just to emphasize that there are important practical insights and values that emerge from direct experience, just as important as those of social science, and we should learn from them. Of course, this is a core lesson of all ethnography, but it pushes against our subtle but pervasive assumption of the superiority of scholarly knowledge. Now, scholarly knowledge certainly has powerful tools, whose value in the struggle should not be naively denied. Yet experience brings important tools and insights also. So, what still remains for further case studies of radical activism, including accompaniment, are detailed accounts and analyses of what scholars and community members bring to each other and how best to put them together.

The other lesson for political struggle is closely related, though not identical. It is vividly expressed by Horton in her chapter in this volume when she remarks on the "transformative potential of accompaniment-as-partnership in contrast to accompaniment-as-navigation. I suggest that when we collaborate with our participants to create political change, accompaniment can transcend the verticality entailed in *doing for* and instead become a form of *doing with*." Doing for and doing with are often not easy to distinguish in practice; as mentioned previously, academics may bring positions, resources, and skills that are much needed, and doing for can well be appropriate in a specific moment. But always maintaining in mind the philosophy of doing with is essential to an equitable and respectful political project. It is the most important lesson of accompaniment.

References

Besteman, Catherine. 2020. *Militarized Global Apartheid*. Durham, NC: Duke University Press.

Campbell, Howard, Jeremy Slack, and Brian Diedrich. 2017. "Mexican Immigrants, Anthropology, and United States Law: Pragmatics, Dilemmas, and Ethics of Expert Witness Testimony." *Human Organization* 76 (4): 326–335.

FitzGerald, David. 2019. *Refuge beyond Reach: How Rich Democracies Repel Asylum Seekers*. New York: Oxford University Press.

Gomberg-Muñoz, Ruth. 2017. "Beyond Il/legality: Persistent Inequality and Racialized Borders of U.S. Citizenship." In *The U.S.-Mexico Transboundary Region: Cultural Dynamics and Historical Interactions*, edited by Carlos Vélez-Ibáñez and Josiah Heyman, 228–243. Tucson: University of Arizona Press.

Heyman, Josiah McC. 2011. "An Academic in an Activist Coalition: Recognizing and Bridging Role Conflicts." *Annals of Anthropological Practice* 35 (2): 136–153.

Heyman, Josiah McC. 2012. "Capitalism and US Policy at the Mexican Border." *Dialectical Anthropology* 36 (2–4): 263–277.

Heyman, Josiah McC. 2015. "Political-Ethical Dilemmas Participant Observed." In *Public Anthropology in a Borderless World*, edited by Sam Beck and Carl A. Maida, 118–143. New York: Berghahn.

Horton, Sarah B. 2020. "Paper Trails: Migrants, Bureaucratic Inscription, and Legal Recognition." In *Paper Trails: Migrants, Documents, and Legal Insecurity*, edited by Sarah B. Horton and Josiah Heyman, 1–26. Durham, NC: Duke University Press.

Lopez, William D., Katherine M. Collins, Guadalupe R. Cervantes, Dalia Reynosa, Julio Salazar, and Nicole Novak. 2022. "Large-Scale Immigration Worksite Raids and Mixed-Status Families: Separation, Financial Crisis, and Family Role Rearrangement." *Family and Community Health* 45 (2): 59–66.

Lopez, William, Nolan Kline, Alana LeBrón, Nicole Novak, Maria-Elena de Trinidad Young, Gregg Gonsalves, Ian Kysel, Basil Safi, and Ranit Mishori. 2021. "Preventing the Spread of COVID-19 in Immigration Detention Centers Requires the Release of Detainees." *The American Journal of Public Health* 111 (1): 110–115.

CHAPTER 10

Putting Accompaniment into Practice

Considerations for Students and Scholars

KRISTIN YARRIS AND WHITNEY L. DUNCAN

One of our aims as we embarked upon this edited volume was to explore, *en conjunto* with our coauthors and collaborators, the various ways that accompaniment takes shape and plays out through our research engagements with im/migrant communities. The chapters in this volume have shared examples and applications of accompaniment in different sites and through various practices. As we mentioned in the introduction, we have welcomed this diversity of approaches, for it illuminates the dynamic, varied nature of accompaniment while also revealing common themes in our work. Holding space for this multiplicity of perspectives, in this final chapter we offer some reflections to help guide our students and colleagues interested in incorporating accompaniment approaches into their work. Rather than a methodological toolkit, this chapter offers touchstones and considerations for reflection as we embark on new projects, renew existing research relationships, develop new collaborations with students and interlocutors, and as we consider shifting community engagements or service work into projects that resemble research (or as we transition research relationships into other forms of relational commitments).

Showing Up and Being-With

Accompaniment is a way of doing ethnography that involves first and foremost showing up alongside our interlocutors—whether we consider those as individuals, organizations, teachers, families, students, friends, community members, or people with the earned expertise of lived experience. As we have seen throughout this volume, showing up can look various ways: convening stakeholder meetings, volunteering on community projects, advocating for public policies, linking people to resources, and writing for, with, or alongside community members. A crucial first step in these engagements is to embody the "practice of presence" (Wilkinson and D'Angelo 2019, 151) and care central to acompañamiento. Like "ethnographic *convivencia*" (Duncan 2018), accompaniment relies on being-with and relationship building through alliances based on trust and reciprocity. This may include discerning and prioritizing what is at stake for any given individual, community, or collectivity that we work with (Kleinman 1995). It may also involve showing up in spaces that are unfamiliar or uncomfortable to us and reflecting on what those feelings of discomfort may have to say about dynamics of power, privilege, and access to resources. This means accompaniment is a dialogic praxis attendant to how we may use our positionalities as students, academics, professors, or researchers in ways that align with community interests and priorities. Sometimes showing up and being-with may result in accompanying processes or interactions that we decide not to classify as research or share with broader publics, as a form of respect for and solidarity with those we work alongside. Other times, showing up means that we are called to use our voice and positionality to share experiences more widely, as we will discuss below.

Addressing Institutional Challenges

Being-with and showing up through accompaniment praxis can thus require deprioritizing or abandoning pre-existing research questions and project plans in ways that may run counter to the incentive structure embedded in academic institutions, disciplines, and careers. On the one hand, this can feel transgressive and empowering; on the other, it can feel frightening and daunting, since our academic livelihoods may depend upon producing widely cited peer-reviewed publications, securing extramural funding, and building a body of work seen as worthy of tenure and promotion using disciplinary and institutional metrics. Further, many of us labor in academic institutions or in departments or disciplines that do not value applied or community-engaged work, which can make accompaniment as a practice of research invisible or render it to an institutionally devalued category of "community service" seen as less rigorous than other forms of institutional labor or academic knowledge production.

As we have engaged in our own dialogues about accompaniment, we have sought to make clear the ways in which our institutional positionalities shape or constrain our abilities to do accompaniment work. It is imperative to be discerning about these external realities and acknowledge when and how accompaniment may or may not be feasible for us as academics, students, and researchers. These apparent tensions between accompaniment and traditional forms of academic research reflect the academy's bias toward colonialist, often extractive, and experience-distant forms of research and rationality that decolonial scholars and activists are working to undo. This undoing is a monumental and essential effort to which we hope our work contributes.

Relatedly, we view engaged research modalities like accompaniment as ways to give substantive meaning to institutional efforts around diversity, equity, and inclusion. Those of us with academic privilege and especially those protected by tenure (as tenure itself is under attack in some places) can call upon our colleagues and universities, our journal and book editors, and our tenure and promotion committees to include accompaniment, activism, advocacy, and other forms of community engagement in job descriptions, tenure and promotion guidelines, as well as in institutional priority and funding decisions. Doing so will help to begin to undo oppressive hierarchies and colonial structures of academia and foster more community-based and community-driven forms of knowledge production.

Making Research Relevant

At the outset of any project or engagement, prioritizing accompaniment may mean shifting focus from developing a priori research questions to building relationships with individuals and communities and developing the trust needed to ask what questions are most pressing for them. A key piece of accompaniment is having clarity about the community we are working with—whether that is a group of individuals with shared experiences based on immigration status, a transnational or a local activist organization, a collective of service providers, or a group of health policy makers. Once we have a sense of our community of engagement, we can consider how our research project might align with or contribute constructively to their work, build capacity among their members or staff, or advance the interest of immigrant justice and inclusion through policy, advocacy, or service provision.

As in *Decolonizing Ethnography* (Bejarano et al. 2019), accompaniment may mean using the research process as an opportunity for capacity building—for instance, through training interlocutors in ethnographic and other research methods, engaging in joint efforts toward community organizing, or embarking on collaborative writing projects. Some chapters in this volume show how accompaniment can mean working together with a community to produce community-relevant health knowledge, gathering testimonios of lived experience of migration-related violence, or supporting students or research participants by connecting them to needed resources. As other chapters in this volume demonstrate, accompaniment can mean that volunteer, service, or community engagements morph into research through processes of ongoing accompaniment—even when "research" was not the initial aim. Whatever the timeline or process, accompaniment requires contemplating if and how research can align with community priorities, and how the products of the research project may elevate community voices and center community experiences.

Acknowledging Power and Positionality

Accompaniment involves a constant reflection around the different positions we may occupy and how power is relatively situated through these positions and our engagements with the communities we work alongside. Through accompaniment praxis, we also become aware of the dynamic ways that power shape-shifts through different contexts and relationships. Some conditions may prompt us to deepen our engagements; at other times, we may need to draw back and reserve our care and emotional labor. Sometimes we may lean into the power we occupy—for instance, when it can be useful to communities to position ourselves as experts or researchers. Other times, we may wish to distance ourselves from our academic or institutional power and foreground our alignment or shared identities with communities. While feminist and Black feminist scholars have long made similar assertions, our contribution to discussions of positionality in engaged research praxis is in part to center the processual and dynamic nature of power through accompaniment. Recognizing our positionality means knowing that our ability to engage in community work, being-with, and advocacy alongside community members may wax and wane with time and that this is acceptable and expected. Throughout this volume, we see examples of authors stepping into and back from their accompaniment engagements. We also have highlighted the important role of building networks of support and solidarity to continue to do this work, to process the emotional involvements this work entails, to step back when needed and let others carry the load, and to prevent burnout over the long term.

Analyses across Multiple Scales

Like ethnography more generally, accompaniment involves participation, observation, and discernment of the ways in which lived experience is shaped by multiple influences: familial, communal, cultural, social, political, economic, historical. The chapters in this volume give examples of this, as accompaniment takes shape in high schools and universities, communities and community-based organizations, activist circles and networks (including those that are transnational and transborder), policy and advocacy work, faith-based communities and testimony, and professional spaces such as applied public health. As we mentioned above, part of accompaniment is delineating the community we understand ourselves to be working alongside; once we have done this, we can begin to assess how dynamics across scales and social processes may shape the experiences of that community. This means that our accompaniment work may start locally or with just one individual, then prompt us into social policy advocacy or activism across national borders. We consider this multi-level approach a strength of accompaniment, even as it requires ongoing reflection about our common goals, areas of divergence and difference, and our commitments to sharing stories and knowledge with different audiences.

Sharing Stories with Broader Publics

A provocation we have collectively embraced in this volume is finding ways to speak to multiple stakeholders and audiences using various writing styles, genres, and voices. Several of our contributors have collaboratively and collectively written their chapters, some have elected to include Spanish language versions of their work, and some have foregrounded the collaborative nature of writing, testimonio, and other narrative forms as modes of accompaniment in and of themselves. While our primary audience for this volume is students, other academics, and a broader public interested in dynamics of im/migration and migrant experiences, most of the contributors to this volume has at different times produced written work or other research projects for a variety of other audiences—whether policymakers, nonprofit organizations, public-sector service providers, families of migrants, activist collectives, and students and their families. We encourage other scholar-activists doing the engaged work of accompaniment to consider the value of multi-vocality when thinking about outcomes of the research process. We envision a future where academia and the humanistic social sciences value oral storytelling, digital media, creative writing, and other narrative and artistic forms of public dialogue as well as peer-reviewed academic publications. As we build that vision of the future of academia, we will continue to think and write together, *en conjunto* with our interlocutors, and to share experiences of im/migration outside of academia in order to shift public perception and hopefully also public policy, as expressions of our accompaniment work.

As we move forward, we will continue to work together to consider new possibilities for engaged ethnographic work and accompaniment with im/migrant communities. So, too, will we continue to grow and elaborate our webs of solidarity, advocacy, and mutual support. We have intended this volume as the beginning of an ongoing dialogue about accompaniment, and we look forward to sharing stories together as we walk alongside im/migrant communities in the years to come.

References

Bejarano, Carolina Alonso, Lucia López Juárez, Mirian Mijangos García, and Daniel Goldstein. 2019. *Decolonizing Ethnography: Undocumented Immigrants and New Directions in Social Science.* Durham, NC: Duke University Press.

Duncan, Whitney L. 2018. *Transforming Therapy: Mental Health Practice and Cultural Change in Mexico.* Nashville, TN: Vanderbilt University Press.

Kleinman, Arthur. 1995. *Writing at the Margin: Discourse between Anthropology and Medicine.* Berkeley: University of California Press.

Wilkinson, Meredith T., and Karen A. D'Angelo. 2019. "Community-Based Accompaniment and Social Work—A Complementary Approach to Social Action." *Journal of Community Practice* 27 (2): 151–167.

AFTERWORD

Acompañamiento // Accompaniment

A SONG BY MIRIAN A. MIJANGOS GARCÍA

Translated by Carolina Alonso Bejarano

Accompaniment is a musical part that is combined with a melody to create a song. As artists who work with music—Mirian as a singer-songwriter and Carolina as a DJ—we see accompaniment as a beautiful and fruitful metaphor for thinking about what ethnography can be and do. This anthology mobilizes accompaniment both as a historically grounded concept and as a poetic possibility—from research method to pedagogical proposal for thinking, organizing, and writing collectively. In doing so, it inspires us to find creative ways to tune in with our comrades, as we continue our activist ethnographic work in the context of patriarchy, xenophobia, racism, and white supremacy.

Acompañamiento // Accompaniment
Acompañamiento tengo todo el tiempo
cuando mis maestros de antropología visitan mi gente
//

At all times I feel accompaniment
when my anthropology teachers visit my people

Esta es la ciencia que estudia la vida
y los cambios fuertes
por fuertes que sean
es de una historia de toda una vida
//

This is the science that studies our lives
and their forces of change
as tough as they may be
The story of a lifetime

No me siento sola y me siento viva
cuando leo libros de los cambios fuertes de un inmigrante
//

I feel alive and not alone
reading books about an immigrant's powerful life changes

Llegan a otros pueblos les cambia la vida
Tienen que adaptarse a otros modales
y hasta más idiomas le son aprendidos
//

They arrive in new towns
their lives altered forever
adapting to new manners and ways of living
and learning even more tongues

No puedo ignorarlos
porque hacen historia
de los cambios fuertes que ofrece la vida
//

I cannot ignore them
because they make history
of the forces of change that life has to offer

Demen un abrazo feliz
Demen un abrazo de paz
Porque si tú eres feliz
la vida más va a brillar
//

Give me a joyful embrace
Give me an embrace of peace
Because the happier you are
the brighter your life will shine

Mi comunidad vive una historia
y antropología es la ciencia viva que estudia la vida
De toda historia
De toda una vida
//

My community is living history
and anthropology is the living science examining our lives
In every history and every lifetime

Demen un abrazo feliz
Demen un abrazo de paz
Porque si tú eres feliz
La vida más va a brillar
//

Give me a joyful embrace
Give me an embrace of peace
Because the happier you are
the brighter your life will shine

ACKNOWLEDGMENTS

The process of writing this volume has itself been an act of accompaniment, solidarity, and care. We wish to thank all our AANIR colleagues for their contributions to this volume—reading and working through your drafts has been enriching and has reminded us of the inspiring power of your work and your various engagements with im/migrant communities. We also wish to thank AANIR members and collaborators whose work is not featured in this volume, but who have been active members of our community nonetheless and thus an ongoing source of motivation and inspiration. In particular, a shout-out to Wendy Vogt for sitting with us at the AAA meetings in Minneapolis in 2016 as we hashed out a nascent vision for our work as anthropologists with migrants and refugees in the face of the onslaught of political attacks that accompanied that presidential election cycle, and which, unfortunately, have not ceased. Wendy helped coin our group's name and our somewhat-clunky acronym, AANIR, and her work with us on several AAA presidential roundtables at anthropology meetings the past number of years has inspired our collective efforts to expand access to higher education for undocumented and DACA-mented students. We also appreciate other colleagues who have collaborated with AANIR over the years in coordinating educational webinars, drafting position papers, sharing teaching experiences, and otherwise using our collective voice as anthropologists of immigration to chart a course of advocacy and justice.

We are grateful to Allyson Carter from the University of Arizona Press. From our initial remote meeting at AAAs in November 2021, with children crying and dogs barking in the background of our Zoom screens, and across the many subsequent challenges ensuing from the COVID-19 pandemic, Allyson believed in this project since its inception. We appreciate the anonymous reviewers and the editorial board at University of Arizona Press for asking pertinent questions, for helping us refine the contributions of this volume, and for pushing the project forward. We also extend special thanks to Alejandra Pedraza for her careful assistance with formatting final versions of this manuscript.

As one reviewer pointed out, a key contribution of this volume has been to approach accompaniment from a variety of perspectives and to demonstrate the potential relevance of this work for other engaged scholars. Yes, accompaniment involves emotional labor and requires us to acknowledge our positionality, including the constraints we face (whether related to time, resources, burnout, caregiving, or institutional demands). But we hope the collective voice of this volume inspires other engaged ethnographers of migration to continue their work in solidarity with im/migrant communities and in critically engaging with what it means to do research in a way that forges bonds of shared struggle, implicating ourselves not just as scholars but as humans in an ongoing process of learning and copresence. Our thoughtful reviewer cautioned us not to appear "superhuman" in our portrayals of this work, and that is certainly not the impression we wish to convey. We have sought to openly discuss our limitations, and we appreciate this opportunity to reflect on our ethnographic engagements in their messiness and human(e)ness.

Our work engaging with im/migrant communities, friends, students, family, and community members has been achieved in contexts of solidarity and community. From our monthly AANIR meetings to shared text threads responding with anger and frustration at the latest executive branch decisions excluding immigrants, we have shared struggles, tears, hopes, and fears over the years. We have relied on the support of the AANIR collective to forge forward. Simply put, we could not have done this work alone. In recognition of the communal nature of this work, we will be donating all proceeds from this book to immigrant-serving organizations on our campuses and in our communities.

Kristin: I would like to thank my wonderful writing group colleagues Maria Fernanda Escallón, Carla Guerrón Montero, and Kemi Balogun for support around writing and for your comments on earlier drafts of the introduction and chapter 5. I am also immensely grateful for Whitney's ongoing coauthorship and camaraderie working through the lifecourse of being an engaged academic alongside all of life's other demands—while trying to stay centered and calm in the face of it all. I drafted chapter 5 while on partial leave from the University of Oregon, during which time I had the opportunity to collaborate with wonderful colleagues in the Community Partnerships Program at Lane County Public Health. I thank those public health colleagues—Ola, Mo, and JW—for pushing my thinking about abolition, white supremacy, and legacies of exclusion in Oregon. I would also like to shout-out friends and *compañerxs* in OCAN, the Cascade Immigration Bond Fund, and Freedom for Immigrants, as well as Karla Schmidt-Murillo at Innovation Law Lab, for your ongoing work advancing immigrant inclusion and justice in Oregon and beyond.

Whitney: I am immensely grateful to all the members of the Denver-based Ni1Más Deportación group for your friendship, bravery, care, and presence. Your conviction that a world is possible in which all humans are afforded rights, dignity, and justice—and your tireless work to realize that world—inspires me daily. My colleagues and students in the Anthropology Department at the University of Northern Colorado are great sources of support and inspiration—thank you for believing in community-engaged and creative work and for being my "anthro-family" for so many years. I would also like to thank Kristin; it has been such a pleasure working with you to pull this volume together and to walk alongside you during this journey. Your solidarity has helped me through some very difficult moments, and your vision, insight, and commitment to advocacy have inspired me to *seguir adelante* time and time again. I would also like to thank my partner, Joel Johnson, whose love, support, and partnership sustain me. And I lovingly thank my little *activistas*-in-training, June and Etta, who inspire me to bring my whole caring self to every endeavor.

CONTRIBUTORS

Carolina Alonso Bejarano is an associate professor of law at the University of Warwick. She is the co-author of *Decolonizing Ethnography: Undocumented Immigrants and New Directions in Social Science* and she is also a DJ and cartoonist.

Anna Aziza Grewe is coordinator for Colectivo Vida Digna, where she supervises international postgraduate interns, coordinates educational programs for young women affected by migration, and works with the families of young unaccompanied migrants returned to Guatemala. She is a popular educator, social worker, and traditional midwife. She holds a bachelor's degree in education from The New School for Social Research/Eugene Lang College and a master's degree in social work from the Columbia University School of Social Work. She completed her studies with the department coordinator of Traditional Midwives from the Western Region of Guatemala and is an accredited midwife. Her areas of expertise span sexual rights, traditional medicine, and pregnancy education.

Alaska Burdette studied anthropology and American studies at the University of Maryland, College Park. She continues to apply her love of learning to her work in mindfulness and study of the natural world.

Whitney L. Duncan is a Colorado-based anthropologist, author, and activist whose creative and academic work centers on immigration and the sociopolitical, cultural, and global aspects of health and emotion. Duncan's book on globalizing mental health practice and cultural change in Mexico, *Transforming Therapy* (2018), won the Norman L. and Rosalea J. Goldberg Prize from Vanderbilt University Press for best book in the area of medicine, and her creative writing has been nominated for the Pushcart Prize. She is a professor of anthropology at the University of Northern Colorado and a founding member of the Anthropologist Action Network for Immigrants and Refugees.

Carlos Escalante Villagran is Maya K'iche, a cultural researcher, and a Mayan spiritual guide. He is the coordinator of Colectivo Vida Digna. Carlos has worked extensively in international trade and marketing of Mayan clothing with widows of Guatemala's armed conflict. He is author of the book *Cosmovisión y Espiritualidad: Meditaciones y reflexiones del pensamiento Maya,* Silabario Ediciones (2016). He served as the research coordinator for the study "Manual de Políticas Culturales: Diversidad cultural, derechos humanos colectivos y construcción territorial en tiempos de 'post' guerra," Editorial Cholsamaj (2010). He holds a bachelor of science degree in economics from the University of San Carlos of Guatemala; a master's degree in rural economics from the University of Lisboa, Portugal; and a master's degree in management for sustainable development from the Instituto Chi Pixab'—Autonomous University of Madrid, Spain.

Christina M. Getrich is an associate professor of anthropology and associate director of the Center for Global Migration Studies at the University of Maryland, College Park. Her teaching and research focus on mixed-status families and immigrant young adults, immigration and health policy, and promoting health equity for structurally marginalized communities. She is the author of *Border Brokers: Children of Mexican Immigrants Navigating U.S. Society, Laws, and Politics* (2019, University of Arizona Press). Getrich has served as a Steering Committee member of the Anthropologists Action Network for Immigrants and Refugees (AANIR) since 2017.

Tobin Hansen is an anthropologist and instructor of social science in Clark Honors College at the University of Oregon. He is a member of the Anthropologist Action Network for Immigrants and Refugees, volunteer at the Kino Border Initiative, and a former fellow at the Center for U.S.-

Mexican Studies at the University of California, San Diego and the Wayne Morse Center for Law and Politics at the University of Oregon. He researches and teaches about social identities, population movements, and state power. Hansen is co-editor of *Voices of the Border: Testimonios of Migration, Deportation, and Asylum* (2021, Georgetown University Press).

Lauren Heidbrink is an anthropologist and associate professor of human development at California State University, Long Beach. She is author of *Migrant Youth, Transnational Families, and the State: Care and Contested Interests* (2014, University of Pennsylvania Press) and *Migranthood: Youth in a New Era of Deportation* (2020, Stanford University Press; published in Spanish with UNAM-CIMSUR, 2021). She was awarded the EU Schuman 70th Anniversary Scholar Award to conduct comparative research on child migration in Greece, Italy, Belgium, and the United Kingdom. She is founder and co-editor of youthcirculations .com and serves as the U.S. board president of Colectivo Vida Digna.

Dan Heiman is an assistant professor of bilingual/biliteracy education at the University of Texas at El Paso, a former elementary bilingual teacher in the borderlands, and a teacher educator at the University of Veracruz. He uses critical ethnographic methods in dual language bilingual education (DLBE) contexts and examines how stakeholders make sense of gentrification processes in these contexts and at times counter them through praxis. He is a co-editor of *Critical Consciousness in Dual Language Bilingual Education: Case Studies on Policy and Practice* (Routledge), which offers vivid snapshots of praxis in DLBE contexts across the United States.

Josiah Heyman is a professor of anthropology and director of the Center for Inter-American and Border Studies at the University of Texas at El Paso. His activism, research, and teaching all center on the U.S.-Mexico border, addressing migration and environmental justice. He is the author or editor of five books and over 160 articles, book chapters, and public policy documents. Two recent works are *Paper Trails: Migrants, Documents, and Legal Insecurity*, co-edited with Sarah Horton (2020, Duke University Press), and *The U.S.-Mexico Transborder Region: Cultural Dynamics and Historical Interactions*, co-edited with Carlos

Vélez-Ibáñez (2017, University of Arizona Press). In 2020, he received the award for Distinguished Achievement in the Critical Study of North America from the Society for the Anthropology of North America.

Sarah Horton is a professor of anthropology at the University of Colorado, Denver. Her research, teaching, public work, and policy activism focus on Latinx immigrants' health disparities, pandemic disparities, health care access, and labor exploitation. She is author of *"They Leave Their Kidneys in the Fields:" Illness, Injury and "Illegality" among US Farmworkers*, which was awarded the Robert Textor and Family Prize in Anticipatory Anthropology in 2017 and received honorable mention for the Society for the Anthropology of North America's 2017 book award. She continues to work with Colorado health care advocacy and immigrant rights groups to reform state health care policy and improve Latinx immigrants' access to care.

Nolan Kline is an assistant professor in the Department of Population Health Sciences at the University of Central Florida College of Medicine. His book, *Pathogenic Policing: Immigration Enforcement and Health in the US South*, was released in 2019, and he is the principal investigator of a study funded by the National Science Foundation focused on LGBTQ+ Latinx activism after the Pulse nightclub shooting in Orlando, Florida. His research uses community-based participatory approaches to respond to fundamental causes of health inequity, such as racism, xenophobia, homophobia, transphobia, and other vehicles of social division. Focusing on political and social determinants of health, his work intersects with public policy and activism.

Lupe López was born in Chiapas, Mexico, to Guatemalan parents. When she was sixteen, she migrated to the United States and has been here for more than twenty years. Lupe came to the United States for the American dream and is living it through her five U.S.-citizen children, who are triumphing in their studies. Since 2013, Lupe has worked as an activist and community leader in the Not1More Deportation sub-group of American Friends Service Committee. She will continue fighting hard for immigrant rights because she loves her people and her community.

Alana M. W. LeBrón is an assistant professor in the Program in Public Health and Department of Chicano/Latino Studies at the University of California, Irvine. As a third-generation Boricua who grew up in south central Texas, Alana leverages community-engaged research approaches to understand how structural racism shapes health inequities for low-income communities of color. Much of her scholarship emerges from partnerships with communities to understand how racism affects the well-being of Latina/o communities and community-driven strategies to interrupt the linkages between racism and health. Alana teaches about how policies, systems, and environments shape health inequities affecting Latina/o communities, community health, and community-based participatory research.

Aida López Huinil serves as the coordinator for the Prevention of Sexual and Gender Violence programs of Colectivo Vida Digna. She develops pedagogical materials for Casa de Aprendizaje Ix Kame, an educational-cultural program, and Kajib' Ix, a model of community mutual support, food sovereignty, and study-practice based on ancestral values and knowledge. She is Maya Mam from Cajolá, Quetzaltenango, a teacher, community organizer, and counselor. She is currently studying psychology at the Mariano Gálvez University in Quetzaltenango, Guatemala. Her work includes coordinating educational trips for international groups, accompaniment of returned migrant children, and the production of audiovisual materials in the Mam language to support migrant communities in the United States.

William D. Lopez is a clinical assistant professor at the University of Michigan School of Public Health, senior advisor at Poverty Solutions, and the author of the book *Separated: Family and Community in the Aftermath of an Immigration Raid* (Johns Hopkins University Press). The child of a Mexican immigrant mother, William uses mixed methods in his community-based research to investigate the impacts of immigration raids while centering the voices of community members who survive and thrive under targeted government surveillance and removal efforts. William teaches about the impacts of immigration enforcement and police violence on individuals, families, and communities and has collaborated extensively with community organizations to make his county a safer, more just place for those of all immigration statuses.

Mirian A. Mijangos García is a singer, songwriter, and naturopath. She is the co-author of *Decolonizing Ethnography: Undocumented Immigrants and New Directions in Social Science*, and she is also a mother, an ethnographer, and an immigrants' rights activist.

Nicole L. Novak is a research assistant professor in community and behavioral health at the University of Iowa College of Public Health. A social epidemiologist and community health researcher, Dr. Novak uses epidemiologic and community-engaged research methods to study structural and policy influences on the health of immigrants, Latinos, and rural residents. Dr. Novak has partnered with multiple community-based organizations to address issues related to health equity in Iowa, including the Center for Worker Justice of Eastern Iowa, the Iowa Harm Reduction Coalition, the Prairielands Freedom Fund, and Iowa Migrant Movement for Justice.

Mariela Nuñez-Janes (profe) is a professor of anthropology and affiliate faculty with the Latino/a Mexican American Studies Program (LMAS) at the University of North Texas. She is a 1.5-generation immigrant Latina who dedicates her career to trying to undo the hurt of U.S. schooling through local research, advocacy, and mentoring that focuses on recovering the cultural assets, funds of knowledge, and navigational capital of Latinx youth and their families. Profe has earned numerous awards and honors for her community-engaged scholarship and mentorship of BIPOC students and faculty. She is the coauthor of *Eclipse of Dreams: The Undocumented-Led Struggle for Freedom*, published by AK Press in 2020.

Ana Ortez-Rivera is a current Master of Public Policy student at Harvard Kennedy School in Cambridge, Massachusetts. She is also a data analyst with Boston Public Schools, where she works at the intersection of data and education policy. Ana graduated from the University of Maryland, College Park, in 2018 with her B.S. in social-cultural anthropology, where she began contributing to the UMD research team with DACA-mented students.

Juan Edwin Pacay Mendoza is the program coordinator for Kajib' Ix of Colectivo Vida Digna. Kajib' Ix is a model of community mutual support, food autonomy, and practical study based on values and ancestral knowledge. Pacay is Maya Tz'utujil from Santiago Atitlán, Sololá, a member of the rural complementary economies research youth committee, family-community organizer, and currently studying agronomy at Universidad Rafael Landívar in Quetzaltenango. His work with Kajib' Ix includes consulting with returned young migrants and their families, working to strengthen family economies and agricultural knowledge based on ancestral knowledge and lunar and solar calendars, planting and use of medicinal plants, and animal husbandry. In addition, he provides educational attention to young people affected by migration and deportation.

Salvador Brandon Pacay Mendoza is Maya Tz'utujil originally from Santiago Atitlán, Sololá, Guatemala. He is a public accountant and auditor specializing in tax law. He has a master's degree in finance. He is the financial coordinator for Colectivo Vida Digna.

María Engracia Robles Robles is the director of education at the Kino Border Initiative, which she co-founded in 2008, in Nogales, Mexico. She earned a bachelor's degree in religious and biblical sciences, has taught classes in educational psychology, and is a missionary sister of the Eucharist. Robles has lived and worked in solidarity with people from marginalized communities in Mexico and Brazil, primarily focusing on grassroots education, including with migrants and deported people in Nogales. She is co-editor of *Voices of the Border: Testimonios of Migration, Deportation, and Asylum* (2021, Georgetown University Press).

Delmis Umanzor graduated from the University of Maryland, College Park, in May 2016 with her B.A. in anthropology and a minor in U.S. Latino/a studies. Delmis is pursuing her master's degree in education policy and leadership at American University. Delmis has served two years as an AmeriCorps VISTA and has worked with one of the most prominent immigrant advocacy and nonprofit organizations in the mid-Atlantic region, providing after-school programming to high school youth. Delmis now works with Prince George's County Public Schools as the community schools coordinator for the International High School at Langley Park.

Erika Vargas Reyes is originally from Mexico and migrated to the United States in 2003, when she was eighteen years old. The mother of three children, Erika has acted as a community leader and organizer in the Denver-based Not1More Deportation subgroup of American Friends Service Committee since 2018.

Kristin E. Yarris is an associate professor of global studies and women's, gender, and sexuality studies at the University of Oregon, where she is affiliated with the Department of Anthropology and the Global Health Program. She is a Steering Committee member of the UO Dreamers Working Group and a co-founder of the Anthropologists Action Network for Immigrants and Refugees. Yarris's first book is *Care across Generations: Solidarity and Sacrifice in Transnational Families* (2017, Stanford University Press). She also is a volunteer affiliated with numerous community and advocacy organizations, including United for Immigrant Justice, Innovation Law Lab, Centro Latinoamericano, and the Oregon Community Asylum Network, and she uses these ties to connect students to opportunities for solidarity, learning, and action.

INDEX